FOR
NOTHING

D0000239

BY **Bill Hull**

Jesus Christ, Disciplemaker

Right Thinking: Insights for Spiritual Growth

Anxious for Nothing

ANXIOUS FOR NOTHING

BILL HULL

Power Books

Fleming H. Revell Company
Old Tappan, New Jersey

Unless otherwise identified, Scripture quotations in this volume are taken from the New American Standard Bible, © The Lockman Foundation 1960, 1962, 1963, 1968, 1971, 1972, 1973, 1975, 1977.

Scripture quotation identified NEB is from The New English Bible. Copyright © The Delegates of the Oxford University Press and the Syndics of the Cambridge University Press 1961, 1970. Reprinted by permission.

Scripture quotation identified NIV is taken from the HOLY BIBLE: NEW INTERNATIONAL VERSION. Copyright © 1973, 1978 by the International Bible Society. Used by permission of Zondervan Bible Publishers.

Library of Congress Cataloging-in-Publication Data

Hull, Bill.
  Anxious for nothing / Bill Hull.
    p.   cm.
  ISBN 0-8007-5258-9
  1. Anxiety—Religious aspects—Christianity.   2. Peace of mind—Religious aspects—Christianity.   I. Title.
BV4908.5.H84   1987
248.8'6—dc 19   87-18444
                                                                   CIP

All rights reserved. No part of this publication may be reproduced, stored in a retrieval system, or transmitted in any form or by any means—electronic, mechanical, photocopy, recording, or any other—except for brief quotations in printed reviews, without the prior permission of the publisher.

Copyright © 1987 by Bill Hull
Published by the Fleming H. Revell Company
Old Tappan, New Jersey 07675
Printed in the United States of America

TO Ed

Contents

Introduction

ED WAS IMPRESSIVE, BUT I KNEW BETTER.

Outwardly, he looked good. Well-dressed and apparently relaxed, he spoke articulately and confidently. It seemed as though he had it all together.

Yet I knew that inwardly Ed was struggling.

I first met Ed when he was going through a period of personal turmoil. It was during that time that he committed his life to Christ. Now he was a faithful church-goer and enthusiastic about his newfound faith.

Underneath the surface, however, Ed was anxiety-ridden. His mind raced with negative thoughts. Often he would feel helpless in the face of the daily barrage of negative thoughts. Day after day he tried to dodge the barrage, and day after day he was defeated. He took medication to moderate the anxiety attacks and still was unable to cope with the inner gnawing that made him miserable. He knew that if he didn't find answers, his anxiety would eventually destroy him.

Then he came to me. Why? I suppose because the other solutions he had received were not working. And also because he wanted to know if God had anything to say about anxiety.

Yes, I assured him, God had something to say. In fact, God had plenty to say about anxiety. And I went on to say that if he would do what God prescribed, he could not only manage his anxiety but he could also have inner peace.

Eighteen months later, Ed was off medication, no longer needed therapy, was experiencing the peace of God, and was quickly becoming a spiritual leader. He completed a discipleship training course, then led a discipleship group of his own. In a word, Ed had become a church leader.

What happened? What happened is what this book is about.

I believe there are millions of people like Ed. Although they have come to know Christ and are committed to Him, many people today—and maybe you are among them—are consistently incapacitated by the blight of anxiety.

When someone asked Him about discipleship, Jesus answered that unless one put God before family, possessions, and self, one could not become His disciple (Luke 14:25–33). I would like to add something else to that: *Unless you have inner peace, you will not be a disciple.*

What I am saying is that your Christian growth will be stunted if it is sidetracked by emotional turmoil. You can waste your entire life struggling with inner conflict; after all, the enemy delights in sabotaging your inner peace. While you have not fallen into deep sin, you have been staggering from one failure to the next.

A staggering Christian is not a victorious disciple. A true disciple is fruitful; his life of joy glorifies God. The bottom line is this: If you are unable to handle anxiety, you will find it impossible to have a vigorous Christian life.

God's prescription for peace can be found between the covers of this volume. It is built around a little more than a paragraph penned by the Apostle Paul. Philippians 4:6–13 contains principles that, when you apply them to your life, will transform your thinking and actions. In fact, Paul said that he had *learned the secret,* the secret of contentment. This book is about that secret and how you can learn it, too.

The Philippian passage will serve as the base of operation. From that base I launch out into related Scripture, psychological observation, and the laboratory of life itself, to make my case.

But I assure you of this: What happened for Ed can happen for you.

It is my hope that it will, indeed, happen for you and that you might enter into the abundant life that Jesus promised (John 10:10).

ANXIOUS FOR NOTHING

one

You Aren't the Only One

ANXIETY IS A NATIONAL CURSE. IT IS WOVEN INTO THE fabric of our lives, it proliferates in our minds, influences our behavior, sets our priorities, ruins our health, and curtails family, career, and spiritual fulfillment.

Poet laureate W. H. Auden once labeled the twentieth century the "age of anxiety." In March 1961, *Time* magazine did a cover story on the place of anxiety in American life. The article said:

> Anxiety seems to be the dominant fact and is threatening to become the dominant cliché of modern life. It shouts in the headlines, laughs nervously at cocktail parties, nags from advertisements, speaks suavely in the

boardroom, whines from the stage, clatters from the Wall Street ticker, jokes with fake youthfulness on the golf course, and whispers in privacy each day before the shaving mirror and the dressing table.

Twenty-five years later, anxiety is more than the dominant cliché. The American eagle is our symbol, the Stars and Stripes is our flag, Francis Scott Key gave us our anthem, and—make no mistake about it—anxiety is our national neurosis.

Anxiety is as American as the New York Yankees, apple pie, and fireworks on the Fourth. Depression, uncontrolled anger, alcoholism, drug abuse, stress, and low self-esteem have their places, but these are still dwarfed by the grotesque gigantism of anxiety. If each pathology listed above is a scoop of ice cream, anxiety is the chocolate sauce that pours over and engulfs them all. A February 1986 study by the National Institute of Mental Health suggests that anxiety has, indeed, arrived as our national emotional pastime.

So if you have anxiety reactions, you are just being a red-blooded American?

Well, yes and no.

When I say yes, I mean that if you have no capacity for anxiety, something is seriously wrong with you.

You see, a certain capacity for anxiety is genetic and is needed for human survival. When you encounter danger, there is a rush of adrenaline, an increased heartbeat, heightened awareness, and increased energy and strength. These are "factory equipment" and if you have them, you are normal. But while your capacity for anxiety is genetic, the amount and forms of anxiety that you have are learned.

Much of your anxiety is a conditional response. Your family, friends, school, church, and business life have shaped your standards of thinking and behavior. Being good means obeying parents, doing well in school, and resisting the temptations of drugs, premarital sex, and rebellion. According to these norms, you should go to college; marry a nice, potentially successful mate; find stability in a starter home; have 2.5 children; go to church; and plan for your children's education and your retirement.

That is engrained in you. You have been conditioned to think that way. However, the degree that you depart from your conditioning usually determines your level of anxiety.

In his book, *Anxiety, The Relationship Between Anxiety and Freedom*, Sören Kierkegaard, the eighteenth-century Danish philosopher and theologian, wrote, "The greater the departure from conventional expectations, the greater the anxiety." Kierkegaard saw anxiety as part of the possibility of freedom. A child learning to walk, riding a bike, going to school; an adult getting married, having children, starting a new job—all of these experiences create anxiety. In fact, any effort to explore, try your wings, test your abilities, will cause anxiety.

Maybe you remember the film *The Jazz Singer*. It was about a talented singer raised in an orthodox Jewish home. The young man wanted to write and sing music that was beyond the pale of his father's approval. The singer underwent a great deal of pain throughout the film because of his inner struggle with his belief system, his love for his father, and his desire to utilize his talent. That inner struggle, that psychological tug-of-war, is exactly what I am talking about. It is the essence of anxiety.

Every day you and millions of others are struggling in a similar way. And it is quite understandable. After all, American culture is dominated by social prestige goals. In business, success is measured in economics. In athletics, success is winning. In the church, success is numerical growth. Success is measured against the productivity of others. In fact, you could say that competitive success is the Holy Grail for measuring self-esteem.

If you are an average American, you are probably thoroughly discipled by your culture. Jesus' words are certainly true: ". . . everyone, after he has been fully trained, will be like his teacher" (Luke 6:40). So it is normal for you, having been shaped by the American culture, to derive your worth and prestige from it.

It's a bit scary, isn't it?

All Americans, even you, have been affected by the "psychologizing of America." The modern gurus are the self-help practitioners, the radio and television psychologists, the get-rich, get-well, get-happy, get-secure experts.

Psychology has become a religion, and people worship at its "truth" daily. America has become a highly analyzed, overtested, introspective society. The line between well and sick has been blurred. You are invited to spend your life preoccupied with self, trying to figure out why you do the things you do and why you think the thoughts you do. Understanding yourself has become both a hobby and a goal, but understanding without direction is of no use.

The psychological community is long on theory and short on answers. The reason for such a predicament is the lack of a solid moral base. Therefore, after insight comes, the solution to behavioral difficulty is up for grabs.

In addition, the *national mind-set* is shaped largely by the advertising industry. If the advertising industry sets the agenda, then television communicates it. Together they form a forceful teaching team. They tell you how you should look, dress, talk, and spend your free time, and where you should eat dinner.

It is the goal of advertising to make you dissatisfied with what you now have and to make you want something you don't have. Advertising is telling you not only that you should have something, but that you ought to have it because you deserve it.

Advertising is in the business of creating expectations.

The difference between this taught expectation and the reality of our lives is what I call the *anxiety space.*

The anxiety space is a place that must be filled. You can fill it with hatred, envy, guilt, resentment, depression, or whatever the enemy can find to make you unproductive. But it is a vacuum that must be filled.

This space, incidentally, is the place that you are warned not to give to the enemy. "Do not give the devil an opportunity" (Ephesians 4:27). The word *opportunity* is from the Greek for "place." So you could translate the verse, "Do not give the devil a place."

When anxiety comes—and it will, because life is crammed with realities that don't meet our expectations—the anxiety space will be filled either by emotional garbage or by the peace of God.

The choice is yours.

The space between your dreams and your daily doings, between your want and your walk, between your reachings and your reality—that's the anxiety space. Advertising has stretched your dreams, your wants, and your reachings, and so in our century the anxiety space has grown enormously. According to the ads, you deserve it all. Yet you don't have it.

How do you respond when you cannot have what you have been taught you deserve? Do you feel your rights have been denied? Are you angry? Are you envious? Do you feel a knot in your stomach because life has dealt you a bad hand?

That's the anxiety space.

What Is Anxiety Anyway?

Definitions of *anxiety* abound. Those from the scientific community could fill a room. Those that can be clearly understood might fill a thimble.

Theologians Paul Tillich and Sören Kierkegaard have distilled the essence of anxiety. Tillich sees it as the threat of nonbeing and Kierkegaard calls it the fear of nothingness. Both definitions focus on death, yet go beyond death. The prospect that, after entrance into the death state, there is nothing, is frightening for the spirit of man, who yearns to live.

But that has nothing to do with *my* anxiety, you say. The end of life may produce anxiety for others, but I'm worried about the end of the month! How do I pay my bills?

Immediate matters like that may seem pedestrian to philosophers, but what gnaws at the rest of us are things like lack of money, retirement, children, relationships, health, and our inability to control bad habits.

A psychologist might define anxiety as "the inner conflict triggered by circumstances that upset my life equilibrium, thus, creating questions about my value, my ability, and my future."

In short, anxiety is the stress created by the difference between *my expectations* and *my reality*. In other words, the *anxiety space*.

You might express it like this: "I expected to be a millionaire by forty; my reality is twenty-five hundred a month." Or, "I expected a loving husband and two obedient children; my reality is divorce and two brats." Or "I expected to be a pro athlete; my reality is church-league softball." Or, "I expected to lose thirty pounds, but I gained ten."

That difference between what was expected and what

happened is the anxiety space that is commonly filled with emotional garbage.

I should also point out that there is a difference between fear and anxiety.

Suppose I am on my way to the dentist's office, fearful and apprehensive. I'm about to have a tooth extracted. On the way I pass a good friend and say, "Hello," but my friend fails to respond. In fact, he looks the other way and ignores me. That creates anxiety. Long after the temporary fear of the tooth extraction is gone, I find myself locked in a struggle, questioning myself and my relationship with my friend. This inner gnawing—this anxiety—goes on for days. It can be vague, at times difficult to identify, but always lurking, sneaking in and out of conscious thought, always trailing an uneasiness that something, somewhere, is wrong.

Sometimes we can talk ourselves out of fear, but fighting anxiety is like boxing our shadows. The harder we try, the more we experience the special feelings that accompany anxiety: uncertainty and helplessness.

I would like to be able to say that Christians are not as prone to anxiety as the general population. I can't say that.

Jesus told His followers, "Do not be anxious then, saying, 'What shall we eat?' or 'What shall we drink?' or 'With what shall we clothe ourselves?' For all these things the Gentiles eagerly seek . . ." (Matthew 6:31, 32). *Gentiles*, in this case, is equivalent to unbelievers, those not committed to Jesus Christ.

His solution to anxiety concerning food, clothing, and health was to put Him and His kingdom first. Then, He said, the other issues of life would slip into their proper places. Jesus did not want His followers to be living like unbelievers, as far as anxiety was concerned.

This is a message even more relevant today than it was in the first century. Instead of being destroyed by anxiety, Christians should be practicing what Jesus taught and should be employing the power that is available.

I know that, you say. I know I should not live an anxiety-ridden life, but how can I help it? I've tried; I've prayed about it many times, but I don't know what I can do about it.

You will remember that earlier I mentioned Paul claimed to have learned the secret of contentment: the peace of God. Let's take a closer look at that secret.

He begins his prescription for peace with the exhortation, **"Be anxious for nothing . . ."** (Philippians 4:6).

According to this verse, how much anxiety should you have?

NONE!

Now wait a minute, you say. What does he mean by *nothing?*

Well, the term *nothing* does seem absolute and too confining. Should there not be a *little* anxiety before speaking to a group, before a piano recital, before the delivery of a speech, before your own wedding? Basketball great Bill Russell would vomit before each game. He then would harness that anxiety and play like the pro he was.

Certainly, there is an anxiety that makes you more productive and improves performance. Productive anxiety is factory equipment and works in your favor. This kind of anxiety is called normal anxiety and *is not* what Paul is talking about.

Paul's word for anxiety is *merimnao*, meaning "to tear apart, to divide." It is an inner struggle that impedes your progress, erodes your positive thinking, reduces productivity, and often debilitates. Psychologists might call it *neurotic anxiety*.

Neurotic anxiety has several characteristics.

1. Overreaction

My younger son used to experience neurotic anxiety with respect to timed math tests. The student is allotted fifteen minutes to complete a number of problems. Normal anxiety would be to experience moderate nervousness, enough to cause excitement, but not enough to debilitate. My son, however, overreacted with such anxiety that he would lose his ability to concentrate. While at home he could do every problem without difficulty; during the test he would miss many problems and sometimes not even finish the exam because of neurotic anxiety.

Many minor situations cause major overreactions. Cartoons depict people jumping on a chair at the sight of a mouse or shooting a roach with a shotgun.

But on a more serious and personal level the most common kind of overreaction is in response to the comments and actions of others. Many people habitually take minor comments to heart and build imaginary reasons for envy, hatred, and bitterness. In response, they may lash out or they may even choose to terminate the relationship entirely. One young mother was hurt and angry because she felt her friend thought she was a poor mother. In reality, the friend had merely suggested that the child might need a jacket because it was getting cool. There was no ulterior motive, no hidden message, but to the neurotic, double meanings are everywhere.

The reason this overreaction is called neurotic is that the victims are frightened by and have a distorted view of reality. The classic definition of a neurotic is one who is afraid of reality. All people are neurotic to some degree. Fear of flying, public speaking, or elevators are all forms of neurosis. The reason people overreact to the opinions of others by lashing out or terminating relationships is that they are more frightened by the truth than by the loss of the relationship. The neurotic misreads the careful critique of a friend as a betrayal; therefore, he avoids the issue by ending the relationship. In fact, some people terminate marriage rather than face the truth they fear so deeply.

2. Redirected Behavior

Redirecting behavior meets two needs in the neurotic. First, if the reality can be repressed, it can be forgotten and will not have to be faced.

Repression is motivated forgetting.

You compensate for the anxiety object by shoving it under the pile of your activity. But relief is temporary. Did you ever try to hold a beach ball underwater? It can be done for a while, but eventually it will roll out and pop to the surface. When you attempt to sit on anxiety objects, invariably they will pop up in a more serious and sometimes perverted form.

A factory worker was fed up with his job. He projected the blame for his poor performance on the inept leadership and the abysmal work environment. He experienced serious anxiety, splitting headaches, stomach problems, and the deterioration of relationships with his work associates, wife, and children. He decided to do something about it, so he organized a work rebellion and called for the resignation of plant leaders.

He did two things wrong. First, he ignored the real problem, which was his inability to do the job. Instead, he repressed what he didn't want to face and busied himself by rebelling against authority. Second, he stored up more resentment. This motivated forgetting will not work. The real issue will submerge, but it will not go away.

A friend took her daughter to buy a pair of shoes. Throughout the selection and fitting, the salesman complained constantly about the store, the poor way the supervisors treated the sales staff, and his dislike for the department store in general. My friend and her daughter finally just walked out. Obviously, the man sold few shoes that day, and just as obviously, the blame went to someone else.

Redirected behavior meets a second need for the neurotic: to project the blame on another person or thing. For the neurotic factory worker it was management. For the unhappy shoe salesman it was his supervisor. For you it may be your children, your spouse, your in-laws, your teacher.

Americans blame the government, Democrats blame Republicans, Republicans blame Democrats, coaches blame officials, fans blame coaches, and players blame both coaches and officials. If you don't want to face the truth, point your finger at someone else. That's the American way.

Repressing the truth and projecting the blame will help you cope with your anxiety today, but it will destroy your world tomorrow.

Why? you might ask.

Because it will return to you in a bigger and stronger form. You have created a Frankenstein. You may enjoy temporary success, but lurking around the corner is a gigantic horror.

3. Ingrained Habits

If you think and behave in ways that avoid reality, you are preparing for a great fall. Ingrained habits of avoidance take over your life and hold you prisoner. You start overreacting to the truth about yourself with negative and bizarre behavior. You find yourself pouring your emotional energy into nonproductive activities such as vendettas and projection of blame. In fact, you are covering up your own inferior performance.

27

After seventeen years, my wife returned to college to study art. She found a surprising attitude among several students. One young woman complained when they did still-life drawing indoors because it was an ugly arrangement—she couldn't draw something that boring. She complained about the outdoor sketching because the teacher wanted a certain type of technique, and she didn't see any reason to try something new.

She resented the teacher's critiques because she had her own style and who was he to say her method was wrong? He showed slides of the masters and discussed their techniques, but they were dead and gone—she came to draw, not look at slides. She resented that she didn't have pretty pictures to take home every day.

My wife tried to explain that many of the classes were exercises; just like a coach puts his athletes through boring calisthenics to be ready for the game, the art teacher trains the eye and hand to see and do certain things. The young woman transferred to another school at midterm, looking for a better art department.

Earlier I said that when you develop a life-style of overreaction and redirected behavior it dominates you, and it takes on a life of its own. It owns you, because your mind is both negative and preoccupied. Anxiety finds its way into every nook and cranny of your thought life. If the business is going well, you worry. If the business is going badly, you worry. Anxiety is floating freely in your mind, controlling you.

Remember, this is a learned behavior and the first two

categories of *overreaction* and *redirection* are the main culprits.

Normal anxiety, then, is Bill Russell vomiting and then going out and playing a great game. *Neurotic anxiety* is Bill Russell vomiting and playing a terrible, tentative game, afraid of making a mistake, immobilized by the opinions of teammates, coaches, and fans. Normal anxiety is being nervous about showing your drawing in class. Neurotic anxiety is blaming your poor work on the teacher, model, light, and so on.

Neurotic anxiety keeps many people, perhaps you, from trying, exploring, growing, and greatness. It is responsible for many heart attacks, cases of shingles, stomachaches, headaches, and depression. It is Public Enemy Number One, sabotaging families, schools, and churches. It is eroding vision and cutting productivity. Christians must learn how to overcome it.

But that is putting it in general terms.

Now, let me be very specific: You must learn the secret.

When Paul exhorts, "Be anxious for nothing," he refers to the inner struggle that cuts into your effectiveness, robs you of joy, and gives you everything from heartburn to colitis.

Nonproductive anxiety is to be avoided.

When someone advocates a certain life-style or solution to a problem, it is wise to check his or her credentials. After all, anyone advocating such ludicrous behavior as not worrying, is akin to *Mad* magazine resident lunatic, Alfred E. Neuman, saying, "What, me worry?" Add to this mad exhortation the two preceding verses and all question is removed. Undoubtedly we are dealing with an armchair theologian.

"Rejoice in the Lord always; again I will say, rejoice! Let your forbearing spirit be known to all men . . ." (Philippians 4:4, 5).

Such unrealistic commands raise questions as to Paul's experience with life in general and anxiety in particular. But it should be remembered that Paul wrote these unrealistic words from prison. Though chained to a Roman soldier, this great theologian was able to pen the above words. Indeed, Paul possessed a secret; indeed, he had learned something that every Christian should learn: the secret to contentment.

Paul did encounter difficulty, and he did not always cope with ease. Paul's casual catalog of catastrophes found in 2 Corinthians 11:23–29 summarizes the rigors of first-century ministry.

> . . . *in far more labors, in far more imprisonments, beaten times without number, often in danger of death. Five times I received from the Jews thirty-nine lashes. Three times I was beaten with rods, once I was stoned, three times I was shipwrecked, a night and a day I have spent in the deep. I have been on frequent journeys, in dangers from rivers, dangers from robbers, dangers from my countrymen, dangers from the Gentiles, dangers in the city, dangers in the wilderness, dangers on the sea, dangers among false brethren; I have been in labor and*

hardship, through many sleepless nights, in hunger and thirst, often without food, in cold and exposure. Apart from such external things, there is the daily pressure upon me of concern for all the churches. Who is weak without my being weak? Who is led into sin without my intense concern?

These are the words of a highly motivated, faithful man. His credentials are impeccable. He had learned to cope with much more pain and opposition than most. But there were times when anxiety hindered his work.

During his second missionary journey Paul came to Troas to meet Titus, one of his disciples. "Now when I came to Troas for the gospel of Christ and when a door was opened for me in the Lord, I had no rest for my spirit, not finding Titus my brother; but taking my leave of them, I went on to Macedonia" (2 Corinthians 2:12, 13).

What happened to Paul happens to you, too. Because of emotional unrest, you can't function effectively. This should encourage you: Paul blew it, too. He was so anxiety ridden as to the whereabouts of Titus, he missed an opportunity. "I had no rest for my spirit." He recognized this and left to look for Titus.

Anxiety often derails our ability to focus on work because we become preoccupied with the anxiety object. Family crises or emergency situations call for total attention, but in day-to-day, normal conditions, inability to concentrate is a sign of serious emotional problems.

Paul is the ideal advocate of being "anxious for nothing." In the first place, he had undergone a great deal of trauma, and trauma teaches; therefore, he was seasoned. Second, he had tried and failed, so he was not advocating something unrealistic. Third, he had emerged from the fire of trauma with a secret that could bring peace and contentment to anyone willing to learn.

Kierkegaard believed that anxiety was a better teacher than reality. You can temporarily evade reality by avoiding the distasteful situation, but anxiety is a source of education always present because you carry it within. Where you go, it goes!

Oswald Chambers said, "All our fret and worry is caused by calculating without God." I agree, but we are imperfect beings and sometimes we will not factor in God. Since anxiety is ever-present in life, our goal is not the elimination of it, but the ability to manage it.

Before you can seriously engage in managing anxiety, you must realize its destructive nature. Scripture abounds with negative descriptions of anxiety. Let's look at three.

1. The Double-Minded Man (James 1:5–8)

The context of James, chapter one, describes the benefits and liabilities of various responses to difficulty. The prescribed form is to consider it all joy, meaning to take the positive view that God will use trouble to build your character, and that in the long run, you will benefit from a good response. A positive response in the face of difficulty gives you the right to call upon God for wisdom (v. 5). You believe God loves you and wants to help. Therefore, you are to ask in faith for wisdom that unlocks the answers to the mystery.

With respect to anxiety, however, we will consider the opposite of faith, which is doubt. It is what James calls the double-minded response, and it is the anxiety-ridden response. James speaks of the negatives of being double-minded.

"But let him ask in faith without any doubting, for the one who doubts is like the surf of the sea driven and tossed by the wind. For let not that man expect that he will receive anything from the Lord, being a double-minded man, unstable in all his ways" (James 1:6–8).

Double-minded means to "look both ways at the same time." You are indecisive and lack conviction. Your favorite color is plaid. You speak in footnotes, not confident enough to claim an opinion for yourself. You get on an elevator, and when the operator asks, "Going up?" you respond, "Yes, if it's not out of your way." James describes such a person as "like the surf of the sea," constantly pulled in different directions.

Perhaps you know what James is talking about. You feel double-minded, unstable. You can't make up your mind; you run hot and cold. One day you are committed, the next, you disappear. You can't seem to lock in on any one thing.

Former Supreme Court justice Oliver Wendell Holmes believed that if a man was to achieve greatness, he would need to be a man of "one idea." That one idea is to drive him and dominate his daily agenda. His idea is built on a bone-deep belief, and he locks in on the goal and spends his life working toward that goal. The double-minded man is unable because he is unstable.

To be unstable and double-minded is to feel helpless, to live a life without direction. It hurts! The most sobering fact is the blunt statement made by James: "For let not that man expect that he will receive anything from the Lord" (v. 7). This is like having God shake His index finger at you saying, "Don't expect anything from Me if you are unstable and double-minded—you will get nothing."

No convictions, no confidence in prayer, baffled by the difficulty in your life, you will listen to the voice of the world rather than the voice of God. You are plagued by competition and comparison. You are torn apart on the inside, riddled with anxiety, and coming up empty again and again.

Perhaps you are one of the scores of Christians wondering why God is holding out. Perhaps you wonder why the blessings of God seem to go to a select few while you go without. According to James, the reason may be a lack of decisive belief. You can't find the courage to act on your convictions. You're miserable, your anxiety space is filled with doubt, guilt, and hostility. That list of emotional garbage, alone, is enough reason to dedicate yourself to the management of anxiety. Your spiritual hands are empty and you feel that your life is a waste. You are experiencing what

James writes: The anxiety-ridden man is the double-minded man and he will get nothing from the Lord.

2. The Cowardly Steward (Matthew 25:14–30)

This parable's context is the passing of the baton of ministry responsibility. The work of reaching the world with the message of Christ is one lengthy relay race beginning with Christ and the apostles. The lesson was drawn from the common occurrence of a wealthy landowner leaving for an extended time and leaving slaves in charge of the work. From the twentieth-century observation deck we clearly see that the landowner is Jesus and the stewards are the apostles and all those who would follow, namely the Church.

The landowner gave his stewards five, two, and one talent and went on a trip. The servant with five turned his into ten; the servant with two doubled his, as well. The servant with one, however, hid his in the ground. The dialogue between the returned master and the resourceful stewards is pleasing to all concerned. The master called them good and faithful, and they were rewarded with greater responsibility and filled with joy.

The master's conversation with the third servant, however, is different and enlightening.

> *And the one also who had received the one talent came up and said, "Master, I knew you to be a hard man, reaping where you did not sow, and gathering where you*

scattered no seed. And I was afraid, and went away and hid your talent in the ground; see, you have what is yours." But his master answered and said to him, "You wicked, lazy slave, you knew that I reap where I did not sow, and gather where I scattered no seed. Then you ought to have put my money in the bank, and on my arrival I would have received my money back with interest. Therefore take away the talent from him, and give it to the one who has the ten talents."

Matthew 25:24–28

The nonproductive servant was frightened. He began his defense with an attempt to project the blame on his authority figure. He accused his master of being unreasonable, a "hard man," as he put it.

When you fail to perform according to an agreed-upon task, do you look for an available scapegoat? If you don't, congratulations, you are indeed rare.

The first tack taken by the anxiety-ridden servant was to call his boss or authority figure inflexible, uncaring, and unreasonable. What makes this so pathetic is that it wasn't a good defense. It was common knowledge that a landowner could take a profit from his land. It was common then and it is common now. It is like a department store employee trying to deflect attention from his ineptness by claiming it is unfair for the owner to take a salary because he doesn't work in the store.

Realizing that such a flimsy excuse was not working, the servant went directly for mercy through self-pity.

"I was afraid, so I hid your talent."

Like many frustrated Christians, he went to God in defeat to beg for mercy—"I'm a special case," they protest. Emotional circumstances make success impossible so they ask God for special grace.

Often God does give a special grace, but this parable is teaching the *consequences of not trying.*

The master did not react with, "Aw, you poor thing, I understand, life is tough and I won't hold it against you."

Abruptly the master pronounced the servant wicked and lazy. Wicked, because he allowed his own doubt and lack of responsibility to stop him from being successful. Lazy, because he didn't try. He could have learned from others; he could have asked for advice. But he simply hid the talent and wasted both time and talent. The master pronounced him wicked and lazy and took the one talent he did possess. The servant was in a worse condition than before.

Anxiety destroyed the man's life. He allowed fear and doubt to tear his mind apart. He was unable to risk, to try, or to be productive, all because of anxiety.

The truth of the matter is that the talent God gives to you is to be used in His service. The modern equivalent of a talent is the spiritual gifts that God has given to all members of His body. The development and employment of these gifts are our birthright and responsibility. *There is no valid excuse for not doing it!*

Your friends may understand the special reasons you give for not utilizing your skills for Christ. After all, you have to make a living, you have children to raise, there are vacations, children's athletics, continuing education. Family, friends, even the pastor of your church may listen to the reasons and find them acceptable. But God does not accept excuses.

He sees through all our well-formed reasons for not serving Him. *Anxiety leads to waste and God hates waste.* The waste He hates most is that of servants throwing their lives away.

Like the servant with one talent, you may be paralyzed by anxiety. You may be fearing the trivial and overlooking the priority of the most important. You may have headaches caused by your boss's expectations and ulcers caused by reactions to your parents. You may fear losing the friendship of neighbors, but a wasted life is far more fearful.

The unproductive servant and the anxiety-ridden Christian follow the same course. They both excuse themselves from the responsibility of living a full and meaningful life on God's terms. The tragic end of the anxiety-ridden life cannot be overstated. The anxiety-ridden person will not get anything from the Lord, and he won't do anything for the Lord. He lacks the faith and the courage.

But there is hope. It's not too late to get started in living a productive life.

3. The Parable of the Thorns (Luke 8:14)

This parable is familiar turf. Four kinds of soil are mentioned, describing four kinds of hearts. Only the fourth soil describes true conversion. The third soil plagued by thorns, however, describes the dynamics of anxiety.

"And the seed which fell among the thorns, these are the ones who have heard, and as they go on their way they are choked with worries and riches and pleasures of this life, and bring no fruit to maturity" (Luke 8:14).

"Choked with worries" describes the "big squeeze." Anxiety about work, materialism, personal peace, and pleasure squeeze the life out of the seeds of truth. Maturity is impossible under such conditions because maturity takes time, and in an atmosphere of anxiety the seeds of truth don't get that time. Anxiety derails progress. There are too many sidetracks, too many captivating sights along the journey to occupy the mind and make reaching the destination impossible. The more external stimuli the anxiety-ridden person receives, the steeper the climb to spiritual goals.

A glut of information bombards our minds. The average American now watches television more than seven hours a day. A flood in Chile, an earthquake in Turkey, a bombing in Beirut, or starvation in Africa—all these contribute to the anxiety issues. Modern man is engaged in a struggle to find a moment for cogent thinking.

There is a hotly contested battle for a piece of time in your mind. Items in the mind are on a "time share" arrangement. Each item gets a certain portion of time. When the seeds of God's Word are planted in your mind, they need enough time to take root and grow into practiced convictions. If they are pushed out, they lie on the surface of your thoughts, but don't take root to create your thoughts.

If you are an anxiety-ridden person you find focusing difficult. Negative thoughts about money, work, or whatever is your current worry, take your mental energy and steal the time needed for the Word to take root. Therefore, you will not commit yourself to the purpose and mission of Christ, which, in turn, makes it impossible for you to answer the call to be a disciple of Christ.

The Word requires you to read, meditate, and memorize God's thoughts. When your inner person is not at rest, and your mind is racing with negatives, you cannot be quiet before God. You cannot sit still and read, talk, watch television, listen to tapes or records; there seems to be no rest for your soul. Francis Schaeffer once lamented, "We have lost our quietness before God." The pedestrian distractions of life make building inner strength an uphill experience.

Why was Paul's exhortation, "Be anxious for nothing"?

Because if you are struggling with anxiety:

1. You will get nothing from the Lord, because you lack faith;

2. You will do nothing for the Lord, because you lack courage;

3. You will commit nothing to the Lord, because you cannot focus.

Finally, because you know that under such circumstances you are not pleasing to God, you rob yourself of joy. Therefore you struggle in misery. This is the worst kind of self-treachery. For you to accept this for yourself is a form of self-loathing.

You can do better.

"Be anxious for nothing" is an exhortation for the eighties and beyond. In a land gripped by introspection, self-will, and high expectations, finding tools to fight anxiety is an imperative.

But remember this: Unless you understand how anxiety can destroy you, you will not change. Only when you find yourself "free-falling" through your anxiety space are you desperate enough to start grasping, reaching, calling out for help.

You start with insight. *Insight* means "to see it as God sees it." One day, because of insight, I committed to lose weight. It was like most other days: I stepped out of the shower and glanced at my figure in the mirror. But for some unexplained reason, that day I saw the fruit of my self-indulgence in a full-length mirror and a moment of great awakening took place. I saw the truth—the fat, ugly, disgusting truth. My body was out of control. It had taken over, and I had become its slave.

I experienced *insight*—I saw what God saw. I saw much more than my body. I saw my lack of discipline;

I saw a person who had given into the flesh and I found it an extremely ugly truth.

Insight alone, however, leads to misery. One of traditional psychology's cardinal "truths" is that coming to know yourself is therapeutic. I believe that coming to insight about the negative side of your nature, without taking action, is worse than not knowing. Indeed, "ignorance is bliss" if there are no plans to change.

Insight into negatives without change leads to guilt. Many Christians suffer from unresolved guilt because they are experts on "ought to's" they are not experiencing. As the maxim goes, "If ifs and buts were fruits and nuts, oh, what a party we would have!" Ifs, buts, should'ves, would'ves, and could'ves are frustrations. My own guilt over the state of my weight was short-lived because I took action.

Insight is absolutely necessary for change. However, insight must team with *repentance* in order for change to take place. They work together as follows:

Let us suppose that I am in a darkroom and my mission is to find a black spot on a white carpet. Since the room is pitch black, my only strategy is to crawl about the room trying to determine by blind touch the location of the dark spot. The mission is hopeless. Even if my hand found the dark spot, I would have no way of knowing it. But if someone would turn on the light, the dark spot would be easy to find.

Insight is the light turned on. The Holy Spirit makes you aware of what needs to be changed. Only by means of the Holy Spirit can you truly see yourself and your sin as God sees it (John 16:8–11; Romans 3:9–14; 1 Corinthians 2:9–16; 2 Corinthians 7:8–10). When you see sin as God sees it, you will desire change.

Sin becomes ugly when its destructive nature is exposed and when the personal damage to your life is realized. There is a good sorrow that comes to your spirit. "For the sorrow that is according to the will of God produces a repentance without regret . . ." (2 Corinthians 7:10).

Insight is God turning on the light and exposing the ugly and destructive nature of anxiety. Sorrow sweeps over you as the implications of such a difficult and wasted life are realized. This leads to a deep desire to change, which leads to repentance.

Repentance is derived from the Greek word *metanoia,* meaning, "after perceiving the facts, I change my mind." Along with the change of mind is the commitment to change. I decided, after my illuminated look into my mirror, to turn away from what I had been doing (following poor eating habits) and start doing something different (eat properly). "I don't want to do that anymore" was my commitment, therefore, I structured my life for change. I didn't need a diet; I needed a new way of eating forever. It took the better part of a year, but I developed new eating habits and lost fifty pounds. Change begins with commitment based upon *insight* and *repentance.*

The focus of this opening chapter is:

1. to clarify the nature of anxiety,

2. to illuminate or to "turn on the light" as to the damage anxiety does to your life, which is destroy effective Christian living, and

3. to convince you to commit to change, to *put off* anxiety and *put on* the solution of God—to fill your anxiety space with God's prescription for peace.

If you desire to manage anxiety, to live a joyful, effective Christian life, pause before reading chapter 2 and ask God to help you see the destructive nature of anxiety in your life. Ask Him to "turn on the light" and then make a commitment to change. In other words, repent of your present course and commit to the change that must take place in order for you to experience joy and meaning in your walk with Him.

Commit yourself to learn the secret of contentment, so that you, too, will be able to say as Paul said, "I can do all things through Him who strengthens me" (Philippians 4:13).

Study Questions

1. Define *anxiety*.

2. What role do insight and repentance play in dealing with the problem of anxiety?

3. What is the difference between productive anxiety and nonproductive anxiety?

4. What is the anxiety space?

5. Give three reasons why anxiety is nonproductive in the Christian life.

6. What are three characteristics that are very common to neurotic or nonproductive anxiety?

two

Everything by Prayer

HIDDEN AWAY IN A HALF-INCH SQUARE ON PAGE 13 OF the January 15, 1986, edition of the *Los Angeles Times* was the notice that President Reagan had decreed May 1, 1986, as a national day of prayer. The space given to and location of this presidential decision indicates its perceived importance to the general public—none.

"What difference does prayer make?" "Oh, well, I guess it can't hurt. If there is a God, He might tune in and do something." The American populace puts prayer in its place, alongside flag-waving and singing the national anthem.

If network and print journalists thought prayer was news, they would cover it. When there is a peace summit, the major networks, wire services, and newspapers dispatch hundreds of journalists to cover the talks. National days of prayer go unreported because few people remember them. Even when remembered, reporters do not cover them and people do not participate. They are not reported on or participated in because they don't seem to work. The day after a national day of prayer seems very much like the day before a national day of prayer.

If prayer is so effective, why does it seem to make so little difference? It's not just the bored populace that asks that question. It's the baptized board member, the Sunday school teacher, the discouraged deacon, the burned-out pastor, and perhaps even you.

Why don't Christians believe in prayer? I define *believe* as doing. Therefore, why don't Christians pray? I define *believe* as making something a regular part of my life. Therefore, why don't Christians make prayer a regular part of their lives?

The secular definition of *believe* is "to accept on an intellectual level." The Scriptures, however, view belief as demonstrated in action. So based on a behavioral level, the question is valid: Why don't Christians believe and, therefore, practice prayer as a way of life?

Christians too often operate in an "experiential vacuum." We don't experience what we say we believe, therefore, our convictions are weak. If they are not translated into experience, these intellectual beliefs won't hold up during pressure situations. When we suffer from experiential ignorance we believe in prayer with our heads, but not with our hearts. Since we haven't prayed consistently, we don't understand it, are not productive in it, and as a result are not excited about it. And certainly we are not selling others on its benefits.

"Experiential ignorance" leads to the worst kind of guilt.

Typically, Christians are educated beyond their level of obedience. Prayer is one of those areas that Christians consider sacred. To oppose it or admit that we don't do it is anathema. For most of us, the knowledge that we don't pray enough is a matter of great anxiety. The expectation is to be a serious person of prayer; the reality is far different. Ironically, prayer is not only fundamental to curing anxiety, neglecting it is a major cause of anxiety among Christians. It wouldn't surprise me if you are disappointed with your prayer life.

Anxiety Is the Problem

Let me reiterate some of what I said in chapter 1, because it is basic to this chapter, as well. When anxiety is present, it tears you apart. It is the inner struggle between expectation and reality, between beliefs and behavior, between cultural values and realistic performance. The gap that separates expectation from reality is the *anxiety space*.

I expected my business to take off after the first of the year; instead, sales took a nose dive. I expected to beat the flu bug by now; instead, I will be out of work another week. Negative emotions such as doubt, fear, and anger all attempt to fill the anxiety space, increasing anxiety, and the struggle is on. Normal anxiety can improve your performance and increase your productivity.

But neurotic anxiety debilitates; it makes you nonproductive, impedes progress, and erodes positive thinking. Worry saturates every nook and cranny. It robs you of joy, and then spiritual growth stops.

Paul's command, "Be anxious for nothing" refers to neurotic, nonproductive anxiety, and it is directed to you.

If you are riddled with anxiety, you will be unable to do anything for the Lord, you will find yourself unable to commit to the Lord, you will find daily life true misery.

Only when you see your sin concerning the tragedy of the past and the bleakness of the future will you be willing to change. When you see it as God sees it, then you will be ready for God's solution.

Prayer Is the Alternative

"Be anxious for nothing, but in everything by prayer and supplication with thanksgiving let your requests be made known to God" (Philippians 4:6).

A simple word association will assist learning. Paul associates *anxiety* with *nothing* and *prayer* with *everything*.

Anxiety/nothing. . . . . prayer/everything.

By employing the small word *but*, he has commanded

an alternative. In verse 6 he has told his readers to have nothing to do with anxiety and everything to do with prayer. To worry about nothing and pray about everything may seem emotionally tantalizing, but illusory. The very belief that life can be lived in a real world without neurotic anxiety is unrealistically optimistic.

But skepticism concerning an anxiety-free life is based primarily on negative experience. The word association above is the suggested formula for release from the debilitating effects of nonproductive anxiety. A word association based on most experience would be reversed. The average person, perhaps even the average Christian, will *worry about everything and pray about nothing.*

When trouble shows its face you worry, fret, get heartburn, lose sleep, chew out the boss, the kids, your spouse, and feel miserable. Then in desperation you say, "Oh, yeah, maybe I should pray." The Christian community has flip-flopped the biblical prescription, not in belief, but in practice. There clearly exists an experiential ignorance with respect to prayer and its ability to cope with the anxiety space.

The choice, however, is clear: pray about it or worry about it. Which will it be?

If we plan to deal with the anxiety space, then we must attack our experiential ignorance with respect to prayer.

There are four major truths concerning prayer and anxiety in Paul's prescription for peace.

1. Prayer Is a Central Work

That is what Paul meant by *everything*.

Many things are central to your life. Eating, sleeping, and grooming are some of the basics. Add those activities that are believed to meet needs or give pleasure, such as exercise, reading, watching movies or television, family fun, talking with friends, and so forth. *Central* means daily—those activities that have become second nature, that are built into your life-style.

Paul advocated adding prayer to the list of activities built into a daily routine. "With all prayer and petition pray at all times . . ." (Ephesians 6:18). "Pray without ceasing" (1 Thessalonians 5:17). The Psalmist encouraged believers to have the praise of the Lord always on the lips. James taught that Christians should pray for one another (James 5:16). Jesus spent the entire night in prayer, the early Church devoted themselves to prayer on a daily basis in their homes, at the temple, in jail and outside of jail. In Colossians 4:2 Paul wrote, "Devote yourselves to prayer, keeping alert in it with an attitude of thanksgiving."

Before prayer can become effective in your battle with anxiety or anything else for that matter, it must be *central* to your daily life.

It needs to become as much of your nature to pray when anxiety comes as to grab your thumb after it has been struck by a hammer. Making it central begins with the fundamental belief that prayer works.

The belief is basic—that God is there, He is interested,

and that things will be different after you have prayed. Without this conviction, it would be more logical to try biofeedback, Primal Scream therapy, or a Jacuzzi; because prayer won't work.

But before you decide to make prayer central to your life, I must issue a warning: Making prayer central will change your life; it will disrupt the bland, but peaceful seas of mediocrity. But without prayer, life simply does not add up. Prayer puts the pieces of life's puzzle together in such a way that is confounding to the unenlightened mind. In order to manage anxiety, *the pieces must come together.* There is no peace without putting the pieces together.

Most Christians consider prayer important like exercise, a proper diet, yearly physicals, dental checkups and flossing. But the daily practice of prayer lays in the corner of your life with the other "ought to's."

If you neglect prayer, you are out of bullets in your battle against anxiety. The Apostle Peter indicated this when he wrote, "Casting all your anxiety upon Him, because He cares for you" (1 Peter 5:7).

A great invitation, it implies that the way you get rid of anxiety is to give it to God. The normal means of communicating with God is prayer.

Prayer, to be everything, must be at the core of daily life. It must be built in to your life-style. If prayer is not made part of your daily routine, it will not become central and will not *touch everything.*

The first step in making prayer central is to believe that prayer is the most effective tool for change. Prayer is not the only thing that can be done, but it is the first thing and the best thing that can be done. Without it you cannot begin to deal with problems. Prayer changes attitudes, heals diseases, secures jobs, removes bitterness, heals wounds, and forgives sins.

Most Christians are ignorant as to what really holds their lives together. People who pray are doing the first and most important thing that needs to be done. For prayer to be everything, you must believe it works and then make it central to your life. Attack the experiential ignorance in your life—start praying.

2. Prayer Is an Intense Work

That is what Paul meant by with "supplication" (Philippians 4:6).

Supplication partly means "a special petition that is deeply desired." Anyone who has prayed during an onslaught of anxiety understands an intense desire for God to act. You may remember a time like that. The word also conveys humility. To *supplement* means to make up for a deficiency; the same root word is used for *supplication*. My synthetic definition is: *Supplication* means to pray with great intensity and great humility during moments of great need.

Only in times of great need do you learn the art of supplication. You are in a free-fall, out of control, working without a net. It is in this context that you can pour out your heart to God in desperation. Praying about objects of anxiety is more about how much of you is in the prayer than how much you pray. Length of prayers do not impress God. Long prayers serve a useful purpose only if there is a great deal to pray about.

Intensity implies depth. Unless the Christian digs deeply, to uncover trouble, real issues are not dealt with. The writer to the Hebrews encourages confident intensity in prayer.

> *For we do not have a high priest who cannot sympathize with our weaknesses, but one who has been tempted in all things as we are, yet without sin. Let us therefore draw near with confidence to the throne of grace, that we may receive mercy and may find grace to help in time of need.*
>
> Hebrews 4:15, 16

When anxiety is tearing apart your emotional fiber, let it out. Go to God with confidence. He understands emotional turmoil. Do not hesitate to tell God what you feel and think; He knows anyway.

Paul's well-known, much-talked-about "thorn in the flesh" is an example of the healthy relationship between the believer and God. In the twelfth chapter of Paul's second letter to the Corinthian church he tells the story of his turmoil. Three times he asked God to remove the thorn and three times God refused. After the third no, Paul became aware of an essential spiritual truth, *God's strength is made complete in man's weakness*. In man's foibles and failures, God finds and takes opportunity to reveal Himself in profound ways.

This truth was born from the womb of intense emotional turmoil. Many miss spiritual insight for lack of intensity and a willingness to grapple with God over the issues. The refusal to "take on God" in prayer is based on the misconception that God will react with anger and malice. What other reason would a Christian have for not shooting straight with God?

While Paul is an excellent example of intensity in prayer, Jesus is a better one. All four Gospels describe Jesus' praying in Gethsemane. Matthew, Mark, and Luke deal specifically with Jesus' struggle. Luke describes the struggle between Jesus' perfect humanity and absolute deity. The struggle was so intense that Jesus sweated great drops of blood. This was true agony, anxiety in the truest sense of the word. He was divided between the natural desire to survive and His divine duty to be sacrificed for the sin of the world.

Jesus experienced a more severe case of anxiety than any man. Here is the perfect polarization of emotion—perfect humanity vying with absolute deity. His humanity was not tainted; there was not the corruption of the flesh that causes the loss of the desire to survive.

The elderly, the weak, the ill, the depressed, the addicted are taking their lives in record number. As society becomes more pleasure-centered, materialistic, nihilistic, and existentialistic, reasons to live continue to wane. Jesus' desire to live was greater than that of any other man who has lived, therefore the intensity of emotion, specifically anxiety, was the greatest ever. At the other pole was the absolute deity and intention to obey His Father and complete His mission.

Luke wrote of Him kneeling and praying fervently. Mark, through Peter's eyes, remembers Him distressed, troubled, grieved, and falling to the ground and crying, "Abba! Father! All things are possible for Thee; remove this cup from Me . . ." (Mark 14:36).

The energy in the voice, the facial expressions, the body language—all combine to describe the intensity. The depth of desire in the request, "remove this cup from Me," is clear from the use of the imperative. This was not a calm, "Okay, if You want to, Father." This was a desperate request, "Father, I want out!" He asked three times and three times His loving Father said, "NO!"

This is not a sanitized, hermetically sealed, stained-glass, ecclesiastically proper prayer. This is a heartfelt request with dirt on it, with sweat on it, with tears on it, with blood on it; *Jesus wanted out!*

Can a spiritual person tell God, "I want out," and not get in trouble? Of course, and the example of Jesus should be reason enough to think it all right. It is normal to want out of difficult situations, to want to survive, to have a pleasant life. There would be something awry if we prayed in a masochistic fashion, asking God to make it tougher so in some sick way we would be more worthy. It is both normal and expected that people pray for health, wealth, pleasure, and for their general well-being. It is a sign of spiritual and emotional health to pray to avoid the difficulties.

We cause much of our own anxiety simply because we are afraid to get intense with God. There is a great release in telling someone our trouble—someone, the only One, who can do anything about it. Even when God says no, simply getting the thoughts and desires from deep within to the mind of God is of great value. It gives us an emotional release valve and increases our intimacy with God.

The perfect Man experienced deep, emotional, ripping anxiety; then in that anxiety, He prayed with intensity, calling from the depths of His heart to have God change the situation. And He did not sin in the process. Shouldn't our prayers be like Christ's?

If you want relief from anxiety, then you must become familiar with prayer, you must make prayer central to your life, and you must weave it into your life-style. The most interesting thing will happen when you pray with this attitude. Even when the request is denied, you will be able to say with Jesus, ". . . not My will, but Thine, be done" (Luke 22:42).

3. Praying Is an Honest Work

That is what Paul meant by ". . . let your requests be made known to God" (Philippians 4:6).

Christians are strange. We believe in a loving, just God who is all-powerful and all-knowing. Yet when we pray, we cover up and are not willing to be honest with Him. We are afraid to tell Him how we really feel. It is strange because we behave as though He didn't already know how we feel or what we think.

This cover-up does not fool God, but we do succeed in fooling ourselves. Often we become angry with God or resent Him for something that He allowed to take place. Instead of coming before Him in honesty, we repress our anger. We won't even admit to ourselves that we are angry with God; we refuse to admit it because we think that it would not be Christian.

I will tell you what is not Christian—to become a "song and dance man" with God. Rather than get to the point in our prayers, we go through a prescribed ritual and speak jabberwocky. God twiddles His thumbs while waiting for us to get to the real reason we are praying, for the punch line. Not only does God not respect such dishonesty, clearly, it is sin.

Jesus pelted the Pharisees with verbal attacks for their superficial approach to the spiritual life. Acting like the Pharisees and becoming a "song and dance man" with God represents a bad example of honesty in prayer, but there are some good examples that deserve attention.

Job was honest with God.

Therefore, I will not restrain my mouth;
I will speak in the anguish of my spirit,
I will complain in the bitterness of my soul.
Am I the sea, or the sea monster,
That Thou dost set a guard over me?
If I say, "My bed will comfort me,
My couch will ease my complaint,"
Then Thou dost frighten me with dreams
And terrify me by visions;

So that my soul would choose suffocation,
Death rather than my pains.
I waste away; I will not live forever.
Leave me alone, for my days are but a breath.
What is man that Thou dost magnify him,
And that Thou art concerned about him,
That Thou dost examine him every morning,
And try him every moment?
Wilt Thou never turn Thy gaze away from me,
Nor let me alone until I swallow my spittle?
Have I sinned? What have I done to Thee,
O watcher of men?
Why hast Thou set me as Thy target,
So that I am a burden to myself?
Why then dost Thou not pardon my transgression
And take away my iniquity?
For now I will lie down in the dust;
And Thou wilt seek me, but I will not be.

Job 7:11–21

David was an honest man as well.

I cry aloud with my voice to the Lord;
I make supplication with my voice to the Lord.
I pour out my complaint before Him;
I declare my trouble before Him.
When my spirit was overwhelmed within me,
Thou didst know my path.
In the way where I walk
They have hidden a trap for me.

Look to the right and see;
For there is no one who regards me;
There is no escape for me;
No one cares for my soul.

Psalms 142:1–4

How refreshing. Get it out—and don't leave anything out! Otherwise prayer becomes nothing more than a song and dance. Without truth nothing is accomplished. These men were upset with God; things were tough and they didn't like it. But both knew God and loved Him; they knew Him fit to serve and were willing to risk telling Him off. Their God was not only fit to love, He could handle some brash and insolent prayers from his unhappy children.

Job was such a model of righteousness that God chose him as a challenge too big for Satan. David was a man gripped by many passions, one being a love for God. David was so desirous of pleasing God that God described him as one after His own heart. If such choice servants model honesty in prayer, Christians would be advised to follow.

What drives too many Christians to prayer is selfishness. Much evangelical praying has degenerated into bringing a daily grocery list before the throne. We request daily benefits and a higher standard of living, with a mountaintop experience thrown in now and then to break the boredom. Like bargain hunters rummaging through a pile of goodies at a garage sale, we are looking for a deal.

The second priority in modern praying is getting God to feel sorry for us and to make things better. This is commonly referred to as self-pity. There is ample reason to feel sorry for oneself. There is always someone with better stuff, more stuff, or newer stuff. Someone is better-looking, younger, richer, has a better job, spouse, or digestive tract. It's so easy to feel sorry for yourself. Please believe me, indulging yourself in a "pity party" will not relieve the problems.

You will only become parasitic to family and friends and finally, pathetic. More important, *God will not fall for it.*

Christians take their self-pity to God and expect Him to respond, "Aw, you poor thing, let Me make things better." Instead of allowing you to continue in such nonproductive activity, God promptly turns the table. He shakes you and gives you His reality and perspective. I think God deals with us in the same way that I deal with my children. I want my children to say what is on their minds, but also I want to help them see why the two motives of "getting the goodies" and "getting sympathy" are nonproductive.

This is the reason you should go to God and tell Him honestly what is on your mind. It will help just to say it out loud. If you are mad at God, say so. If you hate someone, don't cloak it behind righteous anger. If you are bitter, don't try to cover up negative feelings.

If you are forty and not nearly where you wanted to be, tell God you are mad at Him. "Hey, God, why haven't You done more to help me?"

My own pilgrimage into prayer is a case in point. My anxiety space was so large that it had enough room for the Grand Canyon, the Golden Gate Bridge, and the national debt.

For several years I had been wanting to write about discipleship, teach discipleship, and build a local church that was a discipleship model. The rationale behind this was good: to glorify God by obeying the Great Commission and to become a credible spokesman for worldwide planting of disciple-making churches. Of course, in order for this to take place, I would need to become a "name," a luminary, to join the constellation of shining stars in Christendom.

My reality was very little exposure or recognition, plus a new, exciting, but fragile church. I used to pick up the phone just to see if it was still working. The mail was just as boring. Where was the limelight? Where were the speaking engagements? Where were the cards and letters? I had so much to share. I didn't seem to be making progress. Why was God withholding His blessing from my work? I would complain to the Lord, "What is wrong, Lord? Why isn't it working? I know this is Your will; why won't You bless me?"

I wasn't being honest! The honest prayer was, "Lord, I am anxiety-ridden because my ego needs are not being met. I want to be well-known and respected. I want to walk into a room and have people whisper, 'There he is.' I want to be an internationally known author / speaker in great demand; I want fame. Even some fortune wouldn't hurt."

What a great day it was when I finally came clean with God. My expectations had been wrong. I wanted a great ministry for me. There would be enough glory for God to have some too, of course, but I really wanted it for *me*. Then I was able to confess it as sin, repent, and turn away from good goals for wrong reasons.

I found simply imitating Jesus and leaving the results to God to be the scriptural approach. If God thought my contribution significant, He would arrange a wider hearing. It was not my business to be concerned about it. With this new outlook, obscurity was no threat, and fame no temptation. My reality was better, the anxiety space was closed, and my anxiety receded.

My expectations are sometimes wrong and when God's Spirit gives insight, I change my expectations and the anxiety space is closed on that particular issue. Other times I can do something to change my reality, which means to work on the anxiety space from the bottom up, rather than the top down.

Often, after correcting false expectations, there still remains a substantial space between those expectations and reality. Reality is easier to change, in many cases, than expectation. My expectation is to make the honor roll; my reality is a C average. If my expectation is reasonable, then I must work to change my reality.

A few years ago I decided to run in a local six-kilometer race. My expectation was to finish, not to win. That was a realistic goal for a man my age, and it took several months of training just to accomplish that. I was surprised at a group of young runners who were prancing around, warming up, and joking about how they had not trained, but were going to race anyway. No problem. The race organizers knew people would race who had not trained properly and for this reason had a small hospital staffed with medical personnel set up near the finish line. I'm sure most of the people lying on those cots had not planned to end up there.

Too much of the time, expectations are false because we are not willing to work and sacrifice to reach them. Anxiety cuts both ways. We have anxiety for a lack of achievement and guilt mixed with anxiety for a lack of work.

Start closing the anxiety space by being honest with God concerning core motives. Try this: Instead of praying, "God, bless my business so I can give more to Your work," pray honestly, "Lord, I want You to bless my business so people will respect me, so I can have financial freedom to do whatever I please when I please. I want success so I can feel I am somebody important."

Be brutally honest.

"Lord, I want that person, I don't care if she is married."

"Lord, I like hating that person."

"Lord, I enjoy gossip."

"Lord, I enjoy being needy in spirit, because people hug me, counsel me, cry with me, and I don't want to lose that!"

"Lord, I'm jealous of their success."

Praying it out loud, facing the real, core thoughts makes it possible for issues to be dealt with honestly. Unless sin is seen as God sees it, there will be no change. Only when the truth comes out from our coming clean with God will there be hope for removing much of anxiety. Both expectations and reality can change, and with the proper change will come relief. Be honest. God respects it and it is the beginning of healing and change.

4. Prayer Is a Learned Work

That is what Paul meant by "practice" in Philippians 4:9.

The lasting benefits of practice will be explained later, but it is enough now to say that in order for any new habit to stick, it will require practice. Unless truth sticks to the life, it cannot be part of the life. The promised result of practice is ". . . the God of peace shall be with you" (Philippians 4:9). For prayer to be part of the daily Christian life, it must be practiced.

The problem is anxiety, prayer is the alternative, and practice is for lasting results.

The first and most important step to managing anxiety is to make prayer a habitual part of your life-style. The choice is between worry and prayer. There is a prescription for peace taught in Philippians 4:6–9. The total prescription has five steps. This chapter ends with the introduction of the first two steps.

The first step in God's prescription for peace is when anxiety strikes, *immediately stop and pray*. This sounds easy, but for those with deeply ingrained anxiety patterns, nothing is harder.

The normal pattern is to worry first, along with all the destructive behavior that goes with worrying. It might occur to you at a later time that you should have tried praying. Such behavior is learned. Frankly, it's a habit. To immediately stop and pray is a habit as well. The first step to beating anxiety is to employ the first step of the solution—prayer.

The way to break the habit of waiting too long before we pray is to become aware that prayer is the available solution. Awareness can help remind you to stop and pray. Other helps are to repeat the phrase *Stop and pray; stop and pray* over and over to yourself. Write yourself notes, or record it on a tape. Repetition will make the words *Stop and pray* take on the prominence of a neon sign within the mind. The goal is for this vital thought to be so prominent that you cannot ignore it or forget it. This programs into your mind the important first step that opens the door to God's peace.

Prayer does not work unless used. Therefore, the crucial first step is to begin to pray in the face of anxiety. This opens the door for many wonderful things besides relief from anxiety. The practice of prayer enhances your relationship to God, and as God responds to your requests, your faith will be increased. Not only will your faith be increased, but others will be helped by the action of God in their behalf because of your prayers.

Step two is *give it to God*. This is another simple idea. In fact, it is so simple that some consider it to be an irrelevant cliché. Indeed, "giving it to God" is a cliché, but for good reason. Many Christians are carrying heavy burdens that need to be given to God.

"Giving it to God" is subsequent to telling God your requests. The scriptural basis is 1 Peter 5:7, "casting all your anxiety upon Him, because He cares for you." Just as the ability to stop and pray is essential to getting a right start against anxiety, the learned skill of transferring the burden from your shoulders to His is critical as well.

May I suggest a visual aid? First I should state what I don't mean by visual aid. I do not mean *visualization* as it is used among occultists. They use visualization as a means of dreaming and speaking visual images into existence. They also use it as a means of guidance. This opens the door for many evil manifestations that find their most sinister results in satanism and black magic.

What I *do* mean is a simple visual exercise based upon Scripture that will aid the person who is praying in getting results. It helps to have a visual image of what you want to imitate. An athletic move, a dance step, a facial expression, or driving a car—possessing a model makes it easier to duplicate. By simply visualizing the hands of God taking the burden from your shoulders, you can experience a sense of relief. I imagine in my mind's eye taking an empty garbage bag and filling it with my anxiety objects. Then I picture myself placing the "anxiety bag" in the capable hands of God. This visual aid helps me unload the weights that hinder my abundant life.

The first two steps of the five-step prescription for peace are *stop and pray*, then *give it to God*. It's a simple start, but it works. Begin today. *Stop worrying and start praying.*

Study Questions

1. What is the alternative to anxiety?

2. What is the clear choice every Christian has when anxiety comes to his or her mind?

3. Why does prayer need to be woven into the fabric of everyday life in order for it to be effective against anxiety?

4. What role does intensity and supplication play in praying about anxiety or anxiety issues?

5. Why is honesty such a vital character trait of effective prayer in relationship to anxiety?

6. How can the problem of experiential ignorance be addressed?

three

With Thanksgiving

CANCER, AND CANCER, AND CANCER. MY MOTHER, MY father, my wife. I wonder who is next in the queue." Speaking of his wife, the same man wrote:

How do they know she is "at rest"? . . . "Because she is in God's hands." But if so, she was in God's hands all the time, and I have seen what they did to her here. . . . If God's goodness is inconsistent with hurting us, then either God is not good or there is no God: for in the only life we know He hurts us beyond our worst fears and beyond all we can imagine. . . .

What chokes every prayer and every hope is the memory of all the prayer [she] and I offered and all the false hopes we had. Not hopes raised merely by our own wishful thinking; hopes encouraged, even forced upon us, by false diagnoses, by X-ray photographs, by strange remissions, by one temporary recovery that might have ranked as a miracle. Step-by-step we were "led up the garden path."

The bitter musings of the unregenerate mind, a skeptic, a cynic, an agnostic? These are the thoughtful words of the twentieth century's greatest Christian apologist, C. S. Lewis. He was locking horns with the providence of God. He was gripped by the reality of grief. (C. S. Lewis, *A Grief Observed*, Faber and Faber.)

At the time, his anxiety space was so gargantuan he could not close it. His expectation and reality were polarized. In previous chapters I have mentioned that the options to closing the anxiety space are *to change either the expectation or the reality.* There are times however, and this case is one of them, when neither the expectation nor the reality can be changed.

The reality was that his wife was dead and he could not change it. His expectation, which he could not help but have, was that she would live. He had lost on both counts, expectation and reality. When the anxiety space cannot be closed, it must be filled. I should say that it *will* be filled, since the law of human emotion requires the vacuum to be filled. If it is not filled with the peace of

God, it will be filled by anxiety, bitterness, anger, resentment, and other negatives.

This is why Paul includes in his imperative to pray, the often-forgotten attitude, ". . . with thanksgiving . . ." (Philippians 4:6). These two little words which make a big difference are easily missed. This is a serious oversight, for the practice of thankfulness is as important as any truth taught in this passage. Without it, the managing of anxiety will be nothing more than wishful thinking.

A thankful attitude will give you staying power during hard times. It will keep you positive and growing throughout your life. It will make it possible for you to bounce back from disappointment.

Paul himself was required to bounce back many times during his thirty years of living on the cutting edge for Christ. His thankful attitude reveals itself at the beginning of the prescription for peace.

"Rejoice in the Lord always; again I will say, rejoice! Let your forbearing spirit be known to all men. The Lord is near" (Philippians 4:4, 5). Add to this his exhortation to the Thessalonians, "In everything give thanks; for this is God's will for you in Christ Jesus" (1 Thessalonians 5:18).

Note the words *always* in Philippians 4:4 and *everything* in 1 Thessalonians 5:18. A thankful attitude, if practiced, can be the constant property of the spiritual person. A thankful attitude is a developed quality and an evidence of spiritual maturity. In this chapter I am asking three questions, and the answers to these questions will help bring thankfulness to your life.

What Does a Thankful Attitude Look Like?

Some people suppose a thankful attitude looks like the proverbial three monkeys, one with his hands covering his eyes who sees no evil, the second with his hands over his ears who hears no evil, and the third with his hand over his mouth who speaks no evil. Being thankful in all things, they say, is unrealistic, Pollyannaish, like being a graduate of the Mary Poppins School of Irrelevant Theology.

Singer/songwriter Ray Stevens recorded a popular tune in the early seventies entitled "Everything Is Beautiful." Everything *isn't* beautiful comes the honest protest; cancer, child abuse, and starvation are not beautiful.

The world, they claim, is far too ugly and depressing a place to act as though it makes sense or is pleasant. They cast their lot with the late philosopher Albert Camus who considered the ultimate question— Why haven't we committed suicide? Enjoy life while you can, when you can, for tomorrow you might be victimized by the ugliness of the world—and probably will.

While the outlook of skeptics is understandable, they are working in the dim light of limited information. God offers a fuller set of information to help people understand both good and evil. The thankful attitude looks like this:

1. A Thankful Attitude Remembers the Good That God Has Done

Thankfulness is a core teaching in both testaments. For the Old Testament believer, the feasts of Pentecost, Passover, and Tabernacles represented the three major celebrations for the people of God. The dominant activity by far during the feasts was remembering. The people remembered, rehearsed, sang, and praised their faithful God through rituals, altars, and symbols. Each activity was pregnant with meaning, designed to help people remember the greatness of God and all He had done.

A good example of such celebrating is found in 1 Chronicles 16:8–12:

Oh give thanks to the Lord, call upon His name;
Make known His deeds among the peoples.
Sing to Him, sing praises to Him;
Speak of all His wonders.
Glory in His holy name;
Let the heart of those who seek the Lord be glad.
Seek the Lord and His strength;
Seek His face continually.
Remember His wonderful deeds which He has done,
His marvels and the judgments from His mouth.

Another festive hymn is Psalm 103.

"Bless the Lord, O my soul; And all that is within me, bless His holy name. Bless the Lord, O my soul, And forget none of His benefits" (vv. 1, 2).

The New Testament gives the same prominence to thankfulness. Paul taught that being thankful was clear evidence of being Spirit-filled.

"Always giving thanks for all things in the name of our Lord Jesus Christ to God, even the Father" (Ephesians 5:20). He also believed that thankfulness should characterize the prayer life. "Devote yourselves to prayer, keeping alert in it with an attitude of thanksgiving" (Colossians 4:2). Paul was thankful for those with whom he worked. "We ought always to give thanks to God for you . . ." (2 Thessalonians 1:3).

The practices of baptism and communion, regardless of tradition, help believers remember: in baptism, what God has done in the believer's life, and in communion, what God accomplished on the cross. The biblical emphasis on thanksgiving is for the benefit of the believer not the ego needs of God.

God has and can exist in a thanksgiving vacuum. God does not feed on praise or perform any better or worse in relation to it. The benefactors of thanksgiving are those giving the thanks.

Let me explain. *The shortest memory is the spiritual memory.* Scripture not only exhorts believers to remember, but warns believers not to forget.

Spiritual amnesia is rampant because it is built into human frailty. When the seeds of God's Word are not given the time and attention needed to take root, as in the parable of the sower, the enemy comes and snatches them away.

Spiritually then, the Christian becomes like the sports

fan—praising one moment, booing the next; holding banquets in a coach's honor one season, demanding his resignation the next.

The status of God in the forgetful believer's mind is as fragile as His last big play under pressure. "What have You done for me lately?" is the attitude. God is faithful again and again, then when we are squeezed into a tight spot, we protest, "Where are You, God? Have You departed from my life? Why are You being so hard on me?"

If God acted every time, on time, according to our schedule, there would be no need for faith. Recently I told my sons I would meet them at home at a certain time to let them into the house. I arrived fifteen minutes late. They had the screens off and were prying at the windows. When they spotted me, they indignantly asked me where I had been and why I was late.

I am seldom late. For thirteen and eleven years, respectively, my sons have known me to be worthy of their trust. It didn't matter to them that I had an excellent track record, that their needs had always been met, that I loved them and would do everything in my power to help them. Their childish, narrow, ungrateful attitudes were built on the sand of forgetfulness. If my sons would have remembered my faithfulness, they would have patiently waited on the front steps, knowing that I would be there soon.

Christians suffer from spiritual amnesia, because they do not build their memory, they do not store God's work in their memory, and they do not stimulate the memory by rehearsing the wonders of God.

God is not the one who suffers, it is you and I. We suffer because when we forget the works of God, we respond to difficulty in an ungrateful, unbiblical manner. Therefore, we lose the immediate help of God and the peace of God. Anxiety and a lack of blessing are the products of such forgetfulness, rather than peace and the action of God.

Therefore, stimulate your memory, keep a journal, make monuments, make plaques and shellac them and hang them in your house if it will help. Train yourself to remember the many things God has done.

It will keep you from bitterness, also from the "down time"—that period of self-pity before we remember God's faithfulness—and allow God to be His faithful Self during hard times.

The benefit of thankfulness that is most obvious is that of joy, being at peace with God and the situation. A thankful attitude *remembers the good that God has done*. But there is more: It *believes in a good God*.

2. A Thankful Attitude Believes in a Good God

Belief in a good God says, "God loves me and has my best interest at heart." Yet many people and events make belief in a good God difficult. There are unwelcome facts of life such as disease, cruelty, crippled children, infidelity, perversion, disaster—a list of horrors no one likes.

God is responsible for what exists. The best theologian, the brightest mind, the master of logic—none of these can release Him from His creative authorship. While Scripture divorces God from any personal responsibility for evil, He did create a system with the possibility of evil. God therefore, while not being the author of evil, is the Architect of a system that could turn sour.

God, being omniscient, knew ahead of time that man would choose evil. Considering this fact, why did He bother to create when so much evil, suffering, and tragedy lay ahead?

This fact and question prompted the British magazine *Punch* to ask the question, "Should God Resign?"

Some claim that He should not, for God is omniscient, but not omnipotent. Therefore, there are numerous events outside of His ability to control. This is the way many modern philosophers attempt to reconcile a loving God and a suffering world. Poor God, He tries so hard, but there is so much to do. While this is intellectually satisfying for some, it leaves us with a God that has limited power and, in my opinion, is not worth loving or serving.

People are not puppets. It would not have been loving for God to have created robots. Puppets and robots do not respond, they do not will anything. God cannot make it rain and not rain in the same space at the same time, neither can He create a creature of choice without at the same time giving it the ability to choose wrongly.

Ninety-nine percent of human suffering comes about

because of man's inhumanity to man: the extermination of 6 million Jews, the slaughter of millions of Christians. Thousands of people starve to death every day.

Many seemingly "natural" disasters are catastrophic because their effects are compounded by greed, selfishness, and evil: governments that will not provide for their people during floods or droughts, who let relief supplies rot rather than allow people from another culture or political persuasion help distribute them; people required to live in homes that collapse and kill them during earthquakes because their economy won't allow them any better life; the hoarding of goods and the greedy attempts of totalitarian governments to control the world demonstrate the lengths that evil men will go to satisfy their egos.

Hitler and fascism, Joseph Stalin and communism, and Mao Tse-tung exterminated 6 million, 50 million, and 80 million innocents respectively. All in devilish attempts to purify the land and rule the world. Since 1946, communist leaders have slaughtered over 120 million people during peacetime, simply because they want to rule the world. Indo-China, Afghanistan, Hungary, Poland, and Cambodia are but a few examples. If the world worked together as a loving community, most human suffering could be eliminated. "Why does God allow this to go on?" many ask. Then they begin to accuse God of being either evil or weak. If He is all-powerful, why doesn't He eradicate evil from the human condition?

The answer is clear. If God were to eliminate evil, as

some suggest, there would be a negative side effect. That side effect is that the elimination of evil requires not only existing evil, but the possibility and potential for evil as well. Since man is the problem, so to speak, creation would need to be destroyed and redone.

The critic might suggest that God simply separate man from his own evil nature. This solution would require God to do two things that would not be possible.

First, He would need to renege on His claims concerning righteousness, justice, and the already-offered solution of sending His only Son as a provision for sin and a solution to the problem.

Second, He would have to alter the human condition so that each human had no choice but to submit to His Lordship and, thus, return all willful creatures to the earlier-hypothesized robot status.

God's solution was, and remains, to provide the *power* to cope with the human condition and *inner peace* to make life's yoke easy, light, and joyful. Add to that the *promise* that the end of life will bring the elimination of evil and eternal bliss. This was all accomplished through His Son, the Lord Jesus Christ.

Many are not satisfied with this answer. They want God to play by their rules, to solve problems based on their limited understanding. They claim that God is a bad Parent because He withholds from His children what they want. Are parents considered bad for withholding cupcakes, candy bars, and other "junk food" from their children?

When our sons were two and a half, and six months

old, my wife, Jane, took them shopping, not by choice, but by necessity. Her usual method was to carry Kris in a shoulder-sling carrier and Bob in the cart. But on this memorable day, Bob escaped while she was getting the cart and began to amble down the aisle. As he picked up speed he took on all the bodily characteristics of a card-carrying toddler—flaying arms, stumbling feet, and bobbing head. She wasn't sure what the results would be, but she knew they would be bad.

To Jane's horror he was headed full-speed and out of control for a glass counter filled with watches and cameras. She started after him calling, "Bobby, stop!" He accelerated. Just a few feet before he was sure to crash into the glass counter, he swerved through a small opening for the clerk's entry and started running the interior circle with glass counters on both sides. Jane grabbed him as he made his first pass by the entry opening and knelt in front of him on the floor.

Still cradling Kris in one arm and holding Bobby with the other, she looked him directly in the eyes and sternly said, "Never run from me again. When I say, 'Stop,' you stop!" Then she turned him around and gave him three swats on his Toddler-sized Pampers. He responded appropriately with bloodcurdling screams. He has always loved drama. Just then, a woman tapped Jane on the shoulder and said in a sweet, syrupy voice, "Dear, I raised six children and never spanked one of them. It is never necessary to hit a child. You can control yourself, if you try." At that point, Jane admits to some unsanctified thoughts concerning the self-appointed counselor.

The woman was accusing Jane of being a poor parent for making her son behave and applying proper discipline.

There are many observers who are unfair and judgmental toward another parent's actions. The onlooker's judgment is flawed because it is taken out of context. Judging a parent's performance by one special situation is like reading three pages from Leviticus and proclaiming the Bible a boring, irrelevant Book.

To accuse God of being a bad Parent is to magnify this principle ad infinitum. To say that humans evaluating God's action are working without enough information is the greatest of understatements.

The fact that God denies or disciplines is a proof of love, not a demonstration of incompetence. Allowing a child everything he or she desires is utter foolishness. God loves His children perfectly, therefore, He handles us perfectly. The fact that life is often difficult should do nothing to discredit this basic Christian belief. In fact, to recognize the difficulty of life is a sign of solid thinking.

Psychiatrist Scott Peck, in his best-seller *The Road Less Traveled*, writes,

> *Life is difficult. This is a great truth, one of the greatest truths. It is a great truth because once we truly see this truth, we transcend it. Once we truly know that life is difficult—once we truly understand and accept it—*

then life is no longer difficult. Because once it is accepted, the fact that life is difficult no longer matters.

Peck also makes a strong point concerning the nature of problems.

Yet it is in this whole process of meeting and solving problems that life has its meaning. Problems are the cutting edge that distinguishes between success and failure. Problems call forth our courage and our wisdom; indeed, they create our courage and wisdom. It is only because of problems that we grow mentally and spiritually.

When faced with the unwelcome facts of life, it is time for the Christian to believe the Bible. "And we know that God causes all things to work together for good to those who love God, to those who are called according to His purpose" (Romans 8:28).

If Christians obey God, that is how Jesus defined loving God. "If you love Me, you will keep My commandments" (John 14:15). Then the promise of Romans 8:28 applies. Please note that the promise does not teach that "we *see* all things working together for good," rather, "we *know*. . . ." This kind of knowing is a faith issue. Walking by faith rather than sight means to know by faith that what is taking place, even though difficult or confusing, God will work out for our best. Faith and experience join hands to make an "experiential knowing" that serves Christians well during difficult days. The longer one walks with God, the more he sees the evidence that this promise is at work in life.

The words of Jeremiah come to mind: "But let him who boasts boast of this, that he understands and knows Me, that I am the Lord who exercises lovingkindness, justice, and righteousness on earth; for I delight in these things, declares the Lord" (Jeremiah 9:24).

" 'For I know the plans that I have for you,' declares the Lord, 'plans for welfare and not for calamity to give you a future and a hope' " (Jeremiah 29:11).

This God is fit to love. He delights both in those who know and understand Him and in displaying justice and doing good for His children. Add to that His desire for His children to have a bright future with success. If your God is not fit to love, you will not give Him your anxiety objects for safekeeping. If He is not fit to love, He is not fit to trust. If there is no one to trust, then neurotic anxiety will be a lifelong millstone around the neck.

I have written before that if you want to know what God is like, then "think Jesus." Whatever you think about God outside of Jesus is wrong. Jesus came to explain God, and if you desire to know how God would respond or think, survey the Gospels to understand Jesus. Such a quest is a delight to God (Jeremiah 9:24).

A thankful attitude *remembers the good God has done*. It also *believes in a good God*. There is however one more trait that characterizes the thankful attitude. *It believes in a sovereign God.*

3. A Thankful Attitude Believes in a Sovereign God

I will not give something I value to someone I do not trust. I want a good bank for my money, a trustworthy friend with whom I can share personal information, and a competent baby-sitter for my children. One consistent violation of this principle is parents giving the car keys to the family teen who has a brand-new driver's license. He simply hasn't had the experience to be able to act properly in every emergency situation, and we know it, but he has to start somewhere. However, before any rational person entrusts another with something of value there must be the basic belief, or trust, that the person knows what he is doing.

Before I will give my objects of anxiety to God, I must believe that He understands my problem and will handle it. Working without this foundation can push one over the edge of rationality into the abyss of insanity. I must believe that He has all things under His control. If all matters are not under His control and there are a few loose ends, and if I am one of those loose ends, then my anxiety is not helped.

Does God understand computers? Can He format a disk? Does He know my account number at the bank so He can make a deposit? These may seem like foolish questions, until we realize that these are the fundamental issues that must be tackled when trusting God. Can I thank God that He has everything under control, that He is orchestrating all things? How you answer these questions will determine your trust level.

The most common problem with trusting God is that after you have stopped and prayed and given the anxiety object to God, the doubts begin.

Does God really know that my house payment is due Thursday? What if that is a loose end? So we take the anxiety object back. God will always give it back if we want it. Then we find ourselves "playing catch" with God. We throw Him the anxiety object, doubt sets in, and He throws it back. This leads to "prayer fatigue," which ends in giving in to old patterns of doubting that derail the new hope of anxiety management. Our trust level must be higher if we are to learn the secret to contentment. Playing catch with God and realizing how fruitless it is will help you in learning the process of peace.

Some believe that creation is out of control. The Christian at peace, however, must believe that God has creation "fenced in." There is a great deal of choice and freedom within the confines of the fence, but nothing is allowed to jump over. Those who have learned the secret believe God orchestrates events and shapes history. He will bring all things to a perfect conclusion. The universe is at His fingertips and at His bidding.

And He made from one, every nation of mankind to live on all the face of the earth, having determined their appointed times, and the boundaries of their habitation, that they should seek God, if perhaps they might grope for Him and find Him, though He is not far from each one of us.

Acts 17:26, 27

For we are His workmanship, created in Christ Jesus for good works, which God prepared beforehand, that we should walk in them.

Ephesians 2:10

And He is the image of the invisible God, the first-born of all creation. For by Him all things were created, both in the heavens and on earth, visible and invisible, whether thrones or dominions or rulers or authorities— all things have been created by Him and for Him. And He is before all things, and in Him all things hold together. He is also head of the body, the church; and He is the beginning, the first-born from the dead; so that He Himself might come to have first place in everything. For it was the Father's good pleasure for all the fulness to dwell in Him, and through Him to reconcile all things to Himself, having made peace through the blood of His cross; through Him, I say, whether things on earth or things in heaven.

Colossians 1:15–20

A thankful attitude is found in people who believe that God has chosen them to live in a certain place, at a prescribed time, encased in the special circumstances of their country, government, and economic conditions and that God holds all things together. The believer's response is to walk in the good works God has prepared for him. The comfort that comes with a belief in God's sovereign control is essential to both a thankful attitude and personal peace.

A thankful attitude remembers the things God has done, believes in the goodness of God, and considers God sovereign and in control. This is why thankfulness is an imperative for the Christian who is struggling with anxiety.

The reverse is true as well. If you do not believe in these basic truths, you will have anxiety problems. A thankful person believes these truths and practices them. Without this base, Christians will not trust in, walk with, or serve their God.

After answering this first question, What does a thankful attitude look like? we must ask the next question.

Why Are Some People Not Thankful?

One reason anxiety is experienced is that there is a conflict with God. The loggerhead is usually over the way that He has or has not done something. The choice, then, is to take the high road built on a positive God concept, that is, love, truth, and justice held in perfect balance. The other choice is, of course, the low road of resentment of God and resistance to His work.

There are reasons why too many take the low road and are plagued by the inability to be thankful.

1. Human Nature

The first reason people are not thankful is because of *man's nature.* Jeremiah was correct, faithful, powerful, and unpopular. His negative congregational response taught him a great deal concerning the darker side of man's nature. He wrote about it, "The heart is more deceitful than all else and is desperately sick; who can understand it?" (Jeremiah 17:9.)

The Apostle Paul agreed that man's unregenerate spirit lacked interest in spiritual issues. "There is none righteous, not even one; there is none who understands, there is none who seeks for God" (Romans 3:10, 11).

Another helpful teaching from Paul is found in his first letter to the Corinthians. "But a natural man does not accept the things of the Spirit of God; for they are foolishness to him, and he cannot understand them, because they are spiritually appraised" (1 Corinthians 2:14).

Man outside of Christ has strong appetites and has no real control of them, for he doesn't understand his own cravings. Apart from the illumination of the Holy Spirit, man had no interest in God or motive for seeking Him. Finally, without the Spirit's help, spiritual truth is beyond man's reach; it all sounds like religious gobble-dygook.

Essentially man is selfish, interested in his own glory and self-aggrandizement. The world revolves around him, he is the center of all things and all things are evaluated in light of his needs. Therefore, the concept of thankfulness is not built into man's basic nature. This look at man's heart without God lies at the core of why thankfulness is not a natural characteristic of man.

2. Our Culture

Another major contributor to a thankless people is the *culture* in which they live. The American public in particular has been duped. The condition of secular America's mind-set reminds me of a story told by British journalist Malcolm Muggeridge. While still a boy he was eating an open-faced bread-and-jam sandwich. A wasp landed on the jelly section and began to enjoy the sumptuous delight. The devious young Muggeridge sliced the wasp in half before it finished its meal. The wasp, however, didn't seem to mind or notice and continued its little feast. The jelly went in the front and came out the end, such as it was. When the wasp finished, it tried to fly away, and to its surprise, nose-dived into the ground never to fly again, never to do anything again.

The wasp, much like contemporary man, was dead and didn't know it. The secular man has been duped by the devil; he is spiritually dead and doesn't know it. He has been effectively programmed by a satanic world system to be ungrateful, selfish, and impatient. He believes he has rights, personal and civil, that must be met. In many cases this is good—the right to a good public education, to get what he pays for, to vote. But there are other rights that modern man is convinced are his that are anti-Christian and create anxiety.

This is the way it works: Advertising creates artificial needs among the public. I deserve a weekend away. I have the right to go for all the gusto, the best of material goods, a new Easter dress, a new car, a birthday present, the latest style of clothes. I need to be happy, to have a satisfying sex life, to have a fulfilling career, to grow as a person. I have a right to be free from rebellious children or an unpleasant family or job. I deserve the best because I am special. If my mate doesn't meet my needs, I'll dump her.

Celebrities have become modern-day evangelists. *Time* magazine critic Richard Schichel wrote, "Celebrities have become the principal source of power in putting across ideas of every kind—social, political, aesthetic, moral." Indeed, celebrities have become the chief agents of moral change in America.

When an all-pro football player or top-ten box office actor tells you to wear certain clothes, watch certain programs, or hold a particular viewpoint, he becomes a powerful persuader. When you are told that you deserve a high standard of living or you have certain rights, but you don't feel you've gotten them, you feel shortchanged, left out, betrayed.

Seemingly innocent factors, like a delectable issue of *Better Homes and Gardens*, create needs, and we then proceed to meet those needs. The door-to-door salesman is a good example of creating artificial needs. He presents the household member with several options. If the salesman had not come to the door, if the household member had been gone, if he had refused to open the door, it is possible that the household member would never have thought of buying that product. How much has been purchased based solely on clever advertising creating artificial need?

In the major cities of this country there are boardrooms filled with fashion executives deciding how America will be dressed next year. If they determine that it will be pink pedal pushers with green socks for women and T-shirts instead of ties with a three-piece Brooks Brothers suit for men, many of us will conform and pay plenty to be considered contemporary. We don't need all the latest fashions, but the media has been effective in convincing us not only that we do, but that we deserve the best.

The sad result is a thankless society. *When people are convinced they deserve what they cannot have, they lose the capacity for thankfulness.*

When we get what we consider our rightful possession after some delay, we complain, "It's about time!" No gratitude, no joy, it takes all the fun out of giving and receiving. It is indeed a bitter cup to drink. Objectively compare your children's attitudes concerning money and material goods to that of yours as a child, before television had its way with our children.

Why are people not thankful? First, because of our nature; second, because of our culture. While man's nature and man's culture influence Christians, it should be known that Christians face a special nemesis.

3. False Teaching

There is a seductive teaching that has swished its way into our churches, both electronic and local. Read what a popular electronic preacher writes.

"I don't think anything has been done in the name of Christ and under the banner of Christianity that has proven more destructive to human personality and, hence, counterproductive to the evangelism enterprise than the often crude, uncouth and unchristian strategy of attempting to make people aware of their lost and sinful condition."

If this man is right, then the Apostle Paul made a serious error in the first five chapters of his letter to the Roman Christians. In those chapters, Paul brilliantly builds a case for the sinfulness of man and the need of a Savior. What does man need a Savior for, what does man need to repent of, unless it is alienation from, hostility toward, ignorance of, and rebellion against God?

What about the first word of the Gospel? John the

Baptist, Jesus, the disciples, Peter on the Day of Pentecost, all began their messages with *repent. Repentance* means "to turn away from," and what is there to turn away from unless it be sin?

The danger of teaching that omits sin is that it reduces man's need for God, for repentance, and cheapens the work of Christ on the cross. It makes man less grateful for what God has done on his behalf; he sees grace less clearly. While there may be a grain of truth in such a comment about the uncouth nature of the presentation of the doctrine of sin, still, the reality of sin must never be reduced or sugarcoated.

C. S. Lewis said, "Heresy is truth taken a little too far." In this case the writer has taken an observation about methodology too far and by doing so, destroyed an essential doctrine, sin: why man needs God.

Another ingredient in this destructive teaching is epitomized in another Christian leader's writing. "By the spoken word we create our universe of circumstances. You create the presence of Jesus with your mouth. He is bound by your lips and by your words."

This dangerous teaching is being proclaimed over the airwaves and from prestigious pulpits, and being published in hundreds of books and periodicals. Here is the core of it and why it is dangerously misleading.

These people are saying that by means of positive talk the believer can force God to take action. The Christian, via faith and knowledge of Scripture, can paint God into a corner. Recently I saw a man teaching this on television. The evangelist asked the two thousand people in attendance to stand and repeat after him, "Body, I will be well in 1986." This was repeated three times. This was followed by, "Mind, I will be discerning in 1986." And then they took out their wallets and spoke three times, "Wallet, you will be full in 1986." No one is against healthy bodies, sharp minds, and full wallets. The belief, however, that merely by talking positively about them you will make it happen is utter foolishness.

Coupled with this teaching is the idea that the opposite is also possible—that negative talk can bring about the very things you do not wish to happen, that you can speak trouble into existence. I have heard proponents of this teaching stop in mid-sentence and shudder that they almost said they were feeling ill and might be catching something. Certainly they would have gotten sick if they had allowed Satan a hold onto them through negative talk.

To believe that somehow God is placed into such a position as to grant our petition, is to make man God and God under the control of man. This creates an environment in which God is expected to come through with the goods, and if He doesn't then either He is mad or the petitioner has done something wrong. Unanswered prayer in this environment warps man's perception of both himself and God. God is an ogre who holds out on His children when angry, and man is guilty because God has withheld His blessing. This rips into a thankful attitude and tears it to shreds.

Another danger of the positive-talk movement is the location of the power base. Positive thinking that is scripturally sound teaches that positive thinking is possible because God provides both the perspective and the power. The positive-talk movement teaches that the power is in being positive, rather than in the Spirit of God.

The belief that by speaking positive things or believing positive things, you will experience positive things is based on poor logic. To think that by speaking and believing this way you can speak positive reality into existence is not proven in general experience. This simply is not true and is not what the Bible teaches concerning thinking positively. Romans 8:28 and Philippians 4:8 both extol the virtue of positive thinking. The facts are, however, that there is difficulty and trouble in life and thinking positively requires a supernatural source when times are hard.

A television teacher described a harrowing experience when a jumbo jet he was traveling on almost crashed. He claimed that the airplane load of frightened passengers should not have been concerned about crashing because he was aboard. How arrogant, to think that we are so irreplaceable to God's program that, solely based on our life, God would save hundreds of other lives. Add to this the reverse angle—that if he had not been aboard, the plane would have crashed and those lives would not have been spared. What about the godly men and women just as vital to God's work who have perished in airplane crashes? Such flagrant ignoring of both life experience and Scripture makes one wonder if such people are in touch with reality.

Anyone can think positively when life is grand. It is the power of God to see the positive in the negative that distinguishes supernatural living from wishful thinking. The "big difference" is that God gives the believer the power and perspective to look at life in a positive manner. To believe that by the power of the mind or speaking certain words we can make God heal someone or create wealth is nothing more than occultic and finds its origin in the mind of Lucifer.

Speaking things into existence is the exclusive right and privilege of God. The big lie has not changed since the Garden of Eden. The serpent told Eve, "You shall be like God." This, of course, came from the father of lies and the one who once claimed, ". . . I will make myself like the Most High" (Isaiah 14:14). These mistaken teachings under the guise of spiritual growth have made it possible for Satan to get Christians once again to try to be like God and usurp God's authority.

Health, wealth, and position in life are things that God has given to some, not all, and are to be considered gifts not rights. God pours out blessings, and when we receive them, we are to be thankful and reminded of His gracious provision. Even to think we could manipulate God or paint Him into a theological corner is to make Him less than He is. God will not abdicate His Lordship to a pompous and presumptuous group of misguided Christians.

If Paul could hear what has infiltrated the Church, he would add another chapter to Galatians. There would be more to explain and more added to his infamous "Let it be accursed" list. Let it be accursed because Christians will not be thankful. Let it be accursed because Christians will be upset with God for withholding a perceived right. Let it be accursed because unthankful Christians will not manage anxiety and will not bounce back from disappointment. Let it be accursed because unthankful Christians turn bitter, stop growing, and waste their lives. Let it be accursed because it is a lie. That is why Paul added, "with thanksgiving" to Philippians 4:7.

Two vital questions have been answered: What does a thankful attitude look like? and Why are some people not thankful? Now a third question that could unlock the most important information of all.

How Can I Develop a Thankful Attitude?

The answer is illustrated for us by a psalmist named Asaph. He started Psalm 73 with the obligatory statement of trust in God. "Surely God is good to Israel, to those who are pure in heart!" Then he admitted some heartfelt doubt: "But as for me, my feet came close to stumbling; My steps had almost slipped" (v. 2).

Why did he almost "lose it" spiritually? Because he allowed circumstances to circumvent his trust; therefore, he lost his thankfulness in a good God.

"For I was envious of the arrogant, as I saw the prosperity of the wicked. For there are no pains in their death; and their body is fat. They are not in trouble as other men; nor are they plagued like mankind" (vv. 3–5).

He lost perspective—the rich don't hurt like I do, struggle like I do, they are arrogant and proud. Asaph could have turned bitter at this point, but he doesn't as a result of taking the proper action.

"When I pondered to understand this, it was troublesome in my sight until I came into the sanctuary of God; then I perceived their end" (vv. 16, 17).

This a spiritual before and after. Before he had God's perspective he was envious and moving toward bitterness. After he had consulted with God, he saw the rich in a different light, even with the ability to pity them enough to care about the dearth of spiritual life among them.

There are two essentials to making that kind of transition. Much in life will be confusing and disturbing unless, like Asaph, you find the key to God's perspective on what surrounds you.

1. To Develop a Thankful Attitude You Must Be Spirit-filled

Paul linked Spirit-filling to thankfulness in the Ephesian letter. "And do not get drunk with wine, for that is dissipation, but be filled with the Spirit" (Ephesians 5:18).

Being thankful is supernatural; it cannot be done on one's own. Spiritual attributes cannot be developed by human means, neither are they endowed. The necessity for spiritual power is self-evident after striving for divine perspective with limited resources. The reason for such ineptness among believers is the blatant ignoring of the Holy Spirit. Christian living demands assistance. There is no way to wire around the need for the Spirit.

The Spirit-controlled life is a profound mystery, yet the "how to" is easy to explain. The issue is control; who controls the believer, the self or the Spirit? Paul's exhortation indicates that God desires all Christians to live a Spirit-controlled life. The great promise of John's first epistle explains, "And this is the confidence which we have before Him, that, if we ask anything according to His will, He hears us. And if we know that He hears us in whatever we ask, we know that we have the requests which we have asked from Him" (1 John 5:14, 15).

Therefore, a simple act of the will triggers God's control. The command is clear, ". . . be filled with the Spirit." The promise is just as clear—when we pray according to His will, the answer is always yes. The means of being Spirit-filled then is a simple act of the will expressed in a serious prayer.

"Father, I desire to be controlled by Your Spirit. I turn from the former ways of my life, I now turn the control of my life over to You to guide me through life."

This prayer is only the beginning. The reason the Christian life in many places is called a "walk" is that it is a moment-by-moment experience. Decisions are made regularly concerning who will control the life at any given time. The Christian is Spirit-controlled on a percentage basis—50 percent, 75 percent, 90 percent, and so on. As the Christian grows, the percentage should increase.

Anxiety management demands a supernatural resource to see the good in the bad and to walk by faith rather than sight. A good God concept is essential for personal peace. Remembering why God is good when things are bad requires a supernatural ability to recall from the submerged spiritual memory the flawless track record of God.

When Jesus promised the help of the Spirit in John 14:26, ". . . He will teach you all things, and bring to your remembrance all that I said to you," he referred to more than preaching sermons or witness. He has promised to resurrect the archives of our minds, to help us keep perspective when, humanly speaking, there is none.

The Spirit-created, long spiritual memory helps fight off the self spirit of our culture.

2. To Develop a Thankful Attitude You Must Be Patiently Obedient

Patience means endurance. This is an active quality, not intended for the fainthearted. Patiently obedient people grow strong because they continue to obey God regardless of emotion or circumstance. Jesus set the standard for love when He told His disciples, "If you love Me, you will keep My commandments" (John 14:15). Those who learn the secret to inner peace are those who, through the Spirit of God, continue to love

God through obedience and wait for Him to produce something good out of something bad.

Pressure does produce good things. Pressure on coal yields diamonds, applied to flower petals, perfume. Pressure applied to the Christian who is patiently obedient yields character, the fruit of the Spirit, and wisdom (James 1:2–5). A meaningful equation is

Spirit-Filled + Time = Spiritual Maturity.

A thankful attitude is developed by Spirit-filled people who have a firm grip on God's goodness and His ability to control events and who possess long spiritual memories. They expect God to work, to turn trouble into victory, and they have the love and determination to patiently endure. This yields a spiritually mature individual who can handle any anxiety object that comes up.

The thankful Christian is like the small boy who was sick in the hospital. He came from a poverty-stricken home and was eating better in the hospital than at home. A glass of milk was offered to him and he was delighted to have it. The nurse returned a few minutes later to take the empty glass away. To the nurse's surprise, 75 percent of the milk was left. She inquired as to why he had not finished the entire glass. His response was revealing: "You mean the whole glass was for me—all this for me?" He was astonished that there would be an entire glass of milk just for him.

Christians should see God's blessings the same way, overwhelmed that He would lavish all the wonderful gifts and graces that He has. *To think, that God would be so inclined to think of me, and then, knowing me, give me such wonderful things.* This thought alone is enough to ponder and give me reason to praise. Thank You, Lord.

> *Be anxious for nothing, but in everything by prayer and supplication with thanksgiving, let your requests be made known to God.*

You would be right to protest at this point, "I want to be thankful. I know I have some problems with that. But I can't throw off years of bad habits in a few days. I need more information and help on how to learn the secret of contentment."

Please be patient, that information is forthcoming. For now, let's review the formula thus far:

1. Stop and pray.

2. Visualize giving your object of anxiety to God.

3. Thank God for what He has done and what He will be faithful to do in the future to work out the difficult situation for His glory and your good.

Study Questions

1. What are three characteristics of a thankful attitude?

2. What does the sovereignty of God (God's control of all of life) have to do with my peace and my willingness to give Him my anxiety object?

3. Why are people in general not thankful?

4. What cultural factors militate against a thankful attitude?

5. What theological teachings have proven to be a serious problem in creating more anxiety than they solved?

6. What are the ways in which a thankful attitude can be developed?

four

The Peace
of God

IT DOESN'T TAKE A SCHOLAR TO REALIZE WE LIVE IN A WORLD plagued by conflict. The *Canadian Army Journal* records that in 5,586 years of recorded history there have been only 292 years of peace. A meager 1.9 percent. There have been 14,531 wars, with 3,640,000,000 killed. Man's search for solutions to conflict is basic to human nature and a consistent fact of history. Prior to Hiroshima, world peace was a simple proposition: take on any and all tyrants, dictators, and megalomaniacs who believed it was their destiny to rule the world.

Since the advent of the nuclear age, the search for peace has been via summits that have yielded many treaties among the major world powers. World peace is important and should be sought. It reduces the risk of nuclear holocaust and makes the planet safer. Therefore, when Gorbachev and Reagan sit down to chat, the world wants to know what they are talking about. The major networks send their best journalists to cover the summit in excruciating detail.

The search for world peace is carefully planned. Before the meetings, decisions are made as to who says what to whom and when. Where to sit, stand, and walk; how to sit, stand, and walk; and what clothing to wear are all carefully orchestrated. Summits are meticulously planned and are executed by a highly trained few—all with the modest goal of trying to manage the tools of destruction.

The common man's search for inner peace, however, is unabated, unplanned, and part of almost every person's daily life. The very fact that you are reading this book indicates that you have an interest in personal peace.

The exponential growth of the self-help industry is evidence that modern man is immersed in a frantic search for inner rest. Everything from self-assertiveness to self-analysis is offered. All of these, good and bad, represent man's search for a better life.

People are pursuing that illusive thing called peace. The children of the anxiety age are grasping for handles to give them stability, an emotional equilibrium. The Catch-22 is that the search itself stimulates anxiety. Will the next piece of information or formula for success bring peace or even greater disappointment?

The Bible has a great deal to say about peace. What it says is clear and easy to understand. It divides peace into two categories: the world's peace and God's peace.

The World's Peace

A serious error is made by many well-meaning Christians who say, "The non-Christian cannot know peace," or, "The world does not offer peace," or, "I don't know how those people can get through such trauma without the Lord. I know I couldn't."

Yet the fact is that thousands of non-Christians do have peace and work through difficulty daily and in some cases better than Christians. Man possesses factory equipment to deal adequately with much that he faces.

The *Challenger* shuttle disaster in January of 1986 is an example. The nation pulled together in support of the affected families. The outpouring of love, empathy, and support gave the grieving families the encouragement they needed. President Reagan led the way in his touching speech to comfort the families at the funeral. Then he rallied the nation behind them by saying, "Their sacrifice will pull us into the future."

There is great resiliency in humans, a spirit of recovery that never ceases to be both amazing and inspirational. Within man there is a capacity to manufacture peaceful conditions.

The world does offer peace. We know this because

Jesus Himself told us it does. "Peace I leave with you; My peace I give to you; not as the world gives, do I give to you. Let not your heart be troubled, nor let it be fearful" (John 14:27).

". . . Not as the world gives. . . ." The world offers many forms of peace. The "guilt bag," a three-dollar mail-order item, is one. It consists of a brown paper bag with the words *guilt bag* stenciled on the side. To use, simply blow into the bag, tie the top, and throw away your guilt. The inventor made millions.

The world's peace is real. It is very often effective and has been adopted and accepted by Christians as coming from God. How many times have you experienced anxiety because something went wrong? You prayed, you cried, you counseled with those you trust. Then God answered your prayers. How do you know? Because things got better, the problem went away. What else went away? Your anxiety, of course! And what turned up on your doorstep? Personal peace. And you thanked God for His peace.

May I suggest that what you experienced was not the peace of God, but rather the world's peace. The reasoning behind my suggestion? The only reason you felt better was because things got better. Your circumstances changed. You did not *learn to cope* with the difficulty, you were not forced to deal with an unchanging problem.

The world's peace is an exciting, well-paying job, a beautiful home, close friends, and interesting places. It's shopping at the best stores with good credit, dinner at elegant restaurants, romantic cruises, walks on the beach, and kids with good grade cards. It's breakfast on your patio with the morning paper and the feel of the sun on your face.

The world's peace is rooted in circumstances, conditions, and facts. The world's peace is great as long as circumstances and conditions are good, but when something turns sour, the world's peace is disrobed as a cheap substitute for God's peace.

How can you tell if you have accepted the world's peace? The world's peace is an "if only" kind of proposition.

If only things were different. If only my boss was kinder. If only my spouse was more caring. If only I had a bigger house. If only I had more money. If only my children would behave. If only I had slimmer thighs and whiter teeth—if only, if only, if only.

An if-only kind of peace is an inferior peace. It's a peace that can be understood, it makes sense, can be explained rationally, and is rooted in circumstances and conditions.

The world's peace is natural because my *expectations* and my *reality* are not in conflict.

I wanted the promotion and I got it. I wanted a million dollars by age forty and I am on schedule. I have great friends. I entered a ten-kilometer run and finished. I have a loving spouse and my children are successful. Things couldn't be better.

When I received word that my first book was to be published, I almost rolled around on the floor with glee.

I had achieved a major goal of my life. I remember the joy and peace I experienced because of that success.

Two years later, after publishing a second book, I received an advance on a third. I was on a roll. The third book I considered to be the most important of the three I had written. I had already spent the advance, and a publishing date was set. It came as a total surprise when, at the last minute, the publisher decided not to release the book.

Just two years earlier I had celebrated with such unabashed glee, now there was frustration, anger, and my internal questioning of my ideas and writing skill. I recall beating my pillow in frustration. The world's peace had let me down. With the first book, the world's peace worked; with the cancelled project, it fell apart.

A great dinner out with friends and who cares what happened at work? Skiing, camping on the beach, or driving to the desert are weekends of carefree adventure that provide that adrenaline rush or calm break. There are many ways to blot out the week's dose of anxiety.

These things do work; they shouldn't be totally rejected as useless. God, in His common grace to creation, has provided various creature comforts and delights. They can serve as a release valve to the pressure and sameness of life. A rest or a change of pace is good. It is not evil to enjoy life's pleasures within a scriptural framework.

The danger, however, is to misinterpret these good experiences and circumstances as an answer to anxiety.

Like the Cookie Monster on "Sesame Street" your

appetite will be insatiable; you will need more and more of whatever it is you use to find relief. One more glass of wine, a faster car, a bigger house, greater danger, greater thrills, and more excitement. Looking for lasting peace in the world is the ultimate cul-de-sac. "There is a way which seems right to a man, but its end is the way of death" (Proverbs 14:12).

People, places, and things are the world's peace. The arsenal being offered the public includes tapes, books, seminars, retreats, video cassettes, radio talk shows, entertainment, and adventurism. But eventually the peace seeker experiences the law of diminishing returns. The disappointment in the superficial and temporary nature of these solutions creates bigger problems than the original angst.

To experience the world's peace is to experience the fruit of your circumstances. The Christian's advantage is that peace is a fruit of the Spirit which rises above circumstance. Self-discipline, joy, and many other positive attributes, including inner peace, are factory equipment resident in the indwelling Holy Spirit.

To rely only on the world's peace is to deny the supernatural nature of God's peace. The world's peace doesn't "take on" the internal issue of the heart. It doesn't offer insight, repentance, and real change from the inside. Expectations and realities are not changed; therefore, relief is temporary. Internal issues must be dealt with by an internal resource that understands and can change the spiritual person. The world's peace is okay—don't dismiss its helpfulness—but you won't need God for it. What we do need God for is included in the following biblical texts.

For the word of God is living and active and sharper than any two-edged sword, and piercing as far as the division of soul and spirit, of both joints and marrow, and able to judge the thoughts and intentions of the heart.

Hebrews 4:12

For who among men knows the thoughts of a man except the spirit of the man, which is in him? Even so the thoughts of God no one knows except the Spirit of God. Now we have received, not the spirit of the world, but the Spirit who is from God, that we might know the things freely given to us by God.

1 Corinthians 2:11, 12

And do not be conformed to this world, but be transformed by the renewing of your mind, that you may prove what the will of God is, that which is good and acceptable and perfect.

Romans 12:2

What does it all mean? God alone discerns the inner sanctum of the mind; God alone can teach the mind; God alone can renew the mind.

Therefore, let's move from our discussion of the world's peace to the study of God's peace.

God's Peace

Let's return to Jesus' promise in the upper room. "Peace I leave with you; My peace I give to you . . ." (John 14:27).

"My peace" uses the possessive pronoun meaning the source is exclusive to God. This is the same peace that is described in our foundational text in Philippians, chapter 4.

> *Be anxious for nothing, but in everything by prayer and supplication with thanksgiving let your requests be made known to God.* And the peace of God, *which surpasses all comprehension, shall guard your hearts and your minds in Christ Jesus.*
>
> *Philippians 4:6, 7*

The peace *of* God is distinct from peace *with* God found in Romans 5:1. The prepositions of peace are important, for they distinguish the judicial standing a Christian has based on the work of Christ from the daily experience of freedom from anxiety. Peace *with* God is the absence of condemnation via justification. The peace *of* God is the absence from neurotic inner conflict via a prayerful process.

The word *peace* has a rich history. The Hebrew word is *shalom*; the Greek word is *eirene*. Attempting to explain the richness of these words by simple definition is like describing a person based on his Social Security number. The fullest meaning is the opposite of anxiety.

The Greek word for anxiety means "to tear apart." The history of *shalom* and *eirene* is to bring things together. Many say that inner peace is best defined by experience: When you have it, you know it; if you don't, it's just as obvious.

Paul's description of God's peace stimulates the mind, for peace itself defies rationality. "And the peace of God which surpasses all comprehension. . . ."

To *comprehend* means to take set of facts, A, and put it together with set of facts, B, and they fit; it makes sense, it computes. The peace of God flys in the face of facts, sensibility, and reason. Like oil and water, Democrats and Republicans, country music and opera, the peace of God and reason don't mix.

To see a person who is at peace when his world is falling apart makes no sense. Even if the difficulty faced seems somewhat trivial.

Recently my wife had an encounter of the strangest kind at a local grocery. It was raining. She spent quite a long time filling up two carts with groceries. She checked her list closely to make sure she had not forgotten anything. She waited in a long line for a long time, sipping a lukewarm cup of coffee, only to find out at the register that she had forgotten her checkbook. Her carts were then pulled off to the side while she dashed home to retrieve the checkbook.

With coffee in hand she headed out the door. As the automatic doors slid open allowing her to go out and a group of ladies to come in, her foot slipped on the wet floor. With a movement as smooth and deliberate as if she had done it on purpose, she threw that cup of coffee squarely into her face. Onlookers gasped, not daring to laugh, not knowing what to do except gape.

With coffee running down her glasses onto her fresh makeup and down the front of her stained blouse, Jane said with a grin, "I also do card tricks." The tension was broken, and she walked with what dignity she could muster into the rain. I'm sure the onlookers' reactions were mixed. Some must have laughed, others thought, *What a trooper*, and some may have said, "I'd be too embarrassed to shop here again."

People respond differently to a variety of situations. Personality differences partly explain why some people have more anxiety than others. But in more serious matters the reasons run much deeper.

That is why so many have so much trouble understanding a positive attitude in a negative situation. Paul singing in jail, a grieving spouse thanking God for His mercy at his or her mate's funeral, praising God after your business fails or when you are evicted from your home. I told you it doesn't make any sense!

God's peace floods your inner person. You focus on God being a good God. He is in control and He's got a great track record. Even in the difficult situation, you can be thankful because you know He will turn the negative into a positive.

Again, the fruit of circumstances must be distinguished from the fruit of the Spirit. The world's peace is rooted in circumstance—in people, places, and things. Remember, peace is a fruit of the Spirit. God's peace is nonsensical, incomprehensible, and supernatural. God's peace is an enigma to the flesh.

But don't expect it to make sense—*expect it to work!*

Lack of Peace With Self: The Major Roadblock to Inner Peace

Another vital prerequisite to inner peace is to be at peace with yourself. The only way that the formula for peace prescribed by Paul will work is if we have set the course of our life in a proper fashion.

Sometimes the anxiety space can be closed or reduced by some simple honesty with yourself. There are three considerations.

1. Are My Expectations Wrong?

First, every person dealing with anxiety must ask himself, *Is my anxiety space the result of the wrong expectations?*

Expectations must be held up to the searching light of God's Word much like a dollar bill is held in the light to test its authenticity. *Are my expectations of the flesh, are they for self-aggrandizement? If I were to change my expectations, would my reality be okay?*

If my expectations are that I will become wealthy or famous or attain a certain station for personal gain, then the expectation needs to be evaluated and adjusted.

As Psalms 75:4–7 says,

I said to the boastful, "Do not boast,"
And to the wicked, "Do not lift up the horn;
Do not lift up your horn on high,
Do not speak with insolent pride."
For not from the east, nor from the west,
Nor from the desert comes exaltation; But God is the
Judge; He puts down one and exalts another.

Therefore, if my expectations are for selfish gain, God cannot be expected to support such endeavor.

2. Are My Expectations Unrealistic?

The second consideration is that perhaps my expectations are *unrealistic*. To expect to run the three-minute mile, to high jump twelve feet, to make a billion dollars is to set myself up for disappointment. A few talented, lucky, or hardworking (probably all three) people have achieved the impossible. But most people need to have challenging expectations with integrity.

A housewife with three preschoolers who expects an immaculate house is going to experience great anxiety. The expectation is unrealistic and the distance from expectation to reality is big enough to sell to land developers. In order to be at peace with oneself, the expectations of life must possess integrity and be realistic.

3. Have I Done All I Can to Improve My Reality?

This third consideration is the flip side of the second. A student expects to get good grades, have full privileges at home, and get the keys to the family car every Saturday night. The reality is poor grades, being grounded, and maybe never driving the family car again. The result is a very large anxiety space.

This bout with anxiety can be brought to a halt with hard work and the determination to earn good grades. The reality can be changed by self-discipline and hard work. It is my observation that a great deal of anxiety, more than I care to mention, could be reduced through some hard work.

I am at peace with myself when my expectations are both realistic and have integrity. And when I have done everything possible to improve my reality.

Now I would like to join the two concepts. The peace of God is incomprehensible. This peace is possible only when I have examined my anxiety space by evaluating my expectations and doing all I can concerning my reality. When I am sure that my anxiety space is legitimate and the incomprehensible peace of God has filled that anxiety space, then I can experience joy.

Peace and joy go hand in hand. Peace is the absence of inner conflict. Joy is an inner sense of well-being when you know that you have done all you can to obey God. Whereas peace is the absence of inner conflict, joy is the absence of guilt or frustration caused by spiritual negligence. Joy is knowing that I am living an obedient life.

Jesus taught His disciples, "These things I have spoken to you, that My joy may be in you, and that your joy may be made full" (John 15:11).

These things were His conditions for living the obedient life, thus proving to be a disciple (John 15:7–10). The inner knowledge that you are obedient contributes greatly to the reduction of anxiety.

Let's say your expectation was to start and own a company that netted a million dollars a year by age forty. Your reality is $3000.00 a month income and $3023.14 monthly expenses and you're forty-two. But you are obedient to Christ. You are meeting the physical and spiritual needs of your family. You have an exciting ministry through your place of business and a camping ministry with teenagers. You work hard, treat your employees right, and give God 10 percent of your income off the top.

Yes, it's true, you haven't met some earlier goals, but you are at peace with yourself and joy fills your life. Therefore, your anxiety space is small. You can experience peace because you can cope with your expectation versus your reality. God loves you and if He wants you to strike it rich He will arrange it (Psalms 75:4–7). You can relax! (Psalms 46:10.) The obedient life is prerequisite to the peace of God. It removes the biggest roadblock of all: unconfessed sin and habitual sin patterns.

There are a great many Christians who crave inner peace yet are not willing to walk daily with Christ. Their prospects for lasting inner peace are strictly in the hands of a benevolent, gracious God. If they get peace, it will be based on God's decision to overrule normal operating procedure. Paul advocates his prescription as a much more reliable road to peace.

The peace of God is not only incomprehensible, it will guard you.

"And the peace of God, which surpasses all comprehension, shall guard your hearts and your minds in Christ Jesus" (Philippians 4:7).

Picture a concrete bunker surrounded by scores of enemy soldiers. You are locked in quiet peace on the inside, although there is conflict on the outside. You are protected by a single soldier so mighty that not one of the enemy soldiers dares attack. That soldier is the peace of God marching guard duty around the believer's life. That lone soldier's identity is revealed by Paul.

"But now in Christ Jesus you who formerly were far off have been brought near by the blood of Christ. For He Himself is our peace . . ." (Ephesians 2:13, 14).

Christ Himself is the peace of God that marches guard duty around our lives. He protects us from the devilish darts that seek to destroy our peace. Paul does not hesitate to employ the metaphor of war when speaking about the inner struggle for peace. The battle is raging and the stakes are high: the joy and productivity of a Christian.

In his Ephesian letter he speaks of the enemy.

"For our struggle is not against flesh and blood, but against the rulers, against the powers, against the world forces of this darkness, against the spiritual forces of wickedness in the heavenly places" (Ephesians 6:12).

Paul commands all Christians to equip themselves for spiritual conflict by putting on "the armor of God." The formula for peace in the midst of an anxiety-producing world is part of that armor. The most graphic illustration concerning the cerebral battle for the allegiance of the believer is also a Pauline invention.

> *For though we walk in the flesh, we do not war according to the flesh, for the weapons of our warfare are not of the flesh, but divinely powerful for the destruction of fortresses. We are destroying speculations and every lofty thing raised up against the knowledge of God, and we are taking every thought captive to the obedience of Christ.*
>
> 2 Corinthians 10:3–5

The real battle is in the mind. The Christian is immersed in an ideological conflict, even if he fails to recognize it. He receives daily input from both the world and, we hope, the Word. The believer forms a defensive posture in order to ward off the satanic salvos, plus an offensive strategy to take prisoners. Daily, the believer is bombarded by the world around him, the flesh inside him, and the devil prowling about him. What he does with these factors determines the outcome of the struggle. If there is no defense against the philosophy of the world, then the mind receives the world's garbage as readily as a funnel receives liquid.

As a boy, I learned to make orange juice by halving the orange, placing one half on the squeezer, and pressing and twisting it until the juice, seeds, and pulp ran into a tray. Then I would take this mixed liquid and pour it through a mesh strainer into a glass. Only the juice could make it through the mesh. All other portions of the orange were strained out. The mind that is spiritual and is being renewed will be forming a *biblical straining system.* Only those thoughts and desires consistent with Scripture will be received by the critical, discerning mind. The imagery used by Paul is that we take captive every thought to the obedience of Christ. The mind that is biblically quick will strain out what is false and harmful.

The peace of God guards our minds from negative thinking patterns, from harmful memories, from anxiety attacks, from the daily bombardment of unpleasant wrenching facts about life. It doesn't eliminate them, it simply protects us from them once we have rejected them as nonproductive and have given them to God in prayer.

The peace of God is experienced more than understood. For it is incomprehensible and supernatural. It will protect you from the destruction of chronic anxiety.

How to Get the Peace of God

It has been clearly established that Christ refers to peace as ". . . My peace . . ." (John 14:27) and Paul refers to it as "the peace of God . . ." (Philippians 4:7). Incomprehensible, nonsensical, supernatural peace is the exclusive property of God. The only way to get it is from God because it is of God. Therefore, access to peace is through God and He makes the rules.

Rule one is plug into the source. When I first purchased the computer I am presently writing on, I unpacked it, took out the manual, and read. Three hours later the computer was together. Carefully I followed each step prescribed by the manual. It didn't work. I could not understand after retracing my steps several times, not skipping anything, why the stupid thing wouldn't turn on. You guessed it; I soon discovered that I had failed to plug it in. Obvious? Yes, but still I missed the obvious.

God's peace is supernatural and it cannot be experienced until you are plugged into the Spirit of God. The Spirit-filled life has undergone a great deal of abuse and "hype." Abuse because Spirit-filling has been made a cure for everything and anything that ails you. Hype so that people think that unless you get environmentally high, "hats and horns," the heavens scroll back, and extraordinary events accompany your filling, there was no filling or at best an inferior filling.

But the name of the game in Spirit-filling is control. Who is in charge when the decision must be made to obey God or disobey God? The Spirit-filled life is mysterious, supernatural, and simple.

Christians are commanded to be filled with the Spirit. "And do not get drunk with wine, for that is dissipation, but be filled with the Spirit" (Ephesians 5:18).

Getting filled with the Spirit is an act of the will. If I desire Christ to control me, all I need to do is ask. At the moment of spiritual birth the Spirit of God takes up residence in my new self (1 Corinthians 12:13; Colossians 1:26; Romans 8:9). In fact, the entire Godhead resides in the Christian (Colossians 2:9; John 14:10–20). Therefore, the difference between the Holy

Spirit's residence in a believer and Spirit-filling is one of control, not amount. You don't get more of the Holy Spirit when you ask Him to control you; He simply controls. Being controlled by the Spirit (i.e., *Spirit-filled*) is a commanded activity. Without question it is the will of God.

The next step, then, is to grab hold of the wonderful promise that God gives in relation to all commanded activity.

"And this is the confidence which we have before Him, that, if we ask anything according to His will, He hears us. And if we know that He hears us in whatever we ask, we know that we have the requests which we have asked from Him" (1 John 5:14, 15).

This is ironclad. The commanded activity is "be filled with the Spirit" and the promise is that anything clearly His will that is requested will get a hearty YES from our heavenly Father. The Spirit-controlled life is commanded and promised to every willing believer. It is a supernatural resource that is simple to get and necessary to have.

Being plugged into the source makes it possible, then, to walk in the Spirit and to appropriate the peace of God. It makes the prayerful practice of the process of peace possible. Playing according to the rules begins with submitting to Christ and allowing His Spirit to guide moment by moment.

The process that is to be practiced, the secret that Paul learned, now expands from the earlier version.

1. Stop and Pray

Nothing is as obvious; very little is more difficult. In order to right the practiced juxtaposition from anxious–everything and prayer–nothing to anxious–nothing and prayer–everything, prayer must be practiced. The first step to God's peace is to immediately pray when the anxiety comes.

Write the words *Stop and Pray* on a card and place it on the sun visor in your car. Carry a card in your pocket or purse; fill your life with reminders to pray first, *before* you worry. This is not trite, this works, but it must be practiced over a period of time for it to become a habit.

2. Give It to God

How trite! is how the critic would respond. Why not something new? Let me explain. The reason "give it to God" is a cliché, is who else can take it, who else has asked for it, and who else could handle it? What are your options? Give it to others in the form of venting frustration. Give it to others who cannot handle it emotionally. Give it to others who would use it against you. Keep it yourself and let it destroy you and those around you. So don't tell me that "give it to God" is trite. It's necessary for survival.

Here is how to do it! After you have stopped to pray, picture yourself giving your anxiety object to God. Financial matters, your children's future, illness, a business project—regardless of the issue, visualize placing it into a garbage bag and handing it to God.

This is not using visualization as practiced by the occult. This is not visualization at all, it is employing your imagination to make your prayer more effective. The prayer is no more effective for God, but it can be for you. Picturing yourself placing the anxiety object into God's hands assists the process.

3. Thank God for His Peace

This step requires you to believe that God's peace will come. It would be helpful to picture Christ marching guard around your mind. Recall the bunker illustration. Christ Himself, who is our peace, is standing guard, protecting our inner person from anxiety.

Thank Him that peace has come, thank Him that He is in control, that He is good, that He is orchestrating your life for His glory and your good.

What If It Doesn't Work?

1. Lack of Faith

In the beginning stages of the battle against anxiety, your major problem is a lack of faith. You stop and pray, give it to God, and thank Him; then immediately question whether this is realistic. Does God know that bill is due Thursday? Does He know your bank account number? In doubt, you take it back. Then you find yourself playing catch with God. You throw Him the anxiety object, you doubt, He immediately throws it back. This can be very tiring and leads to frustrating defeat.

In order for the process to work, you must believe that what God says is true. A story is told that during World War II a young boy was trapped on a roof while German bombers blitzed London. The boy's father ran to his assistance and told the boy to jump. Frightened by the dark, the boy cried out, "I can't see! I can't see!" The father replied, "But I can see you, now jump." The boy trusted his father and jumped to the safety of his arms.

Like the boy, when you give your anxiety object to God, you can't see how He can help. But like the boy, you must jump, or trust that what your heavenly Father says is trustworthy.

Take the plunge, believe!

2. Something More Negative Happens

Just when you say things can't get worse, they do! You get a parking ticket, you're late for work, you miss the important presentation of your project. You stop and pray, give it to God, thank Him for marching guard duty around your life, and the phone rings. It's your mother and she's broken her leg and wants you to take off work for a month to take care of her.

These things do happen. Yet they are just temporary setbacks, and by determination they can be overcome.

In fact, such events can force you to learn the process much more quickly. So don't give up when you take quick successive hits from the world, the flesh, and the devil.

3. Physical Problems

If severe anxiety plagues you, one of the first curative steps is a physical exam. There are people who do all the right things spiritually and still suffer from anxiety. Chemical imbalances, hormonal irregularities, food allergies, prescription drugs—all these can strongly alter the emotional state. For example, there are more physical reasons for depression than emotional ones. Don't overlook your body's condition as a major factor in anxiety, for we are psychosomatic beings.

4. Conflict With Others

Much of this subject is addressed earlier in the "Peace With Yourself" section. An unforgiving spirit, the root of bitterness, will block your way to the peace of God. This roadblock must be removed by repentance, confession, and the refreshing forgiveness of God. Unless unresolved conflict is dealt with (Matthew 5:23, 24; Matthew 18:15–18), peace will remain just beyond your grasp.

5. Second-Nature Issues

Deeply ingrained negative thinking patterns are by far the most common cause of anxiety. Not only are deeply embedded attitudes the greatest cause, they also are the hardest to overcome. Years of "sameness" in thinking and acting have "grooved" the mind so that, like a phonograph playing a flawed record, the needle is stuck in that groove. Many actions are taken without thinking, without a need to think. As naturally as you grab your thumb after striking it with a hammer, you think negative thoughts when certain stimuli activate your mind.

Overcoming patterns of thought is a great challenge. But it must be done, it can be done, and God has promised in Paul's prescription for peace that He will make it possible.

These five roadblocks are the most common reasons the prescription presented thus far does not work. The remaining chapters will teach how you can overcome these roadblocks and learn the secret of attaining peace.

Study Questions

1. What is the world's peace? Give three examples. How can you determine if you have settled for the world's kind of peace?

2. Why is the world's peace easy to attain and just as easy to lose?

3. What bearing does the fact that peace is the fruit of the Spirit have on the entire discussion of the supernatural aspects of peace?

4. What is God's peace in relationship to what Jesus said in John 14:27 and what Paul said in Philippians 4:7?

5. Explain the difference between *happiness* and *joy*.

6. Name two primary means by which we can get God's peace.

7. Name the first two steps in the process of peace, God's prescription for peace.

8. Name the five reasons why, after you have prayed and given it to God, the prescription for peace might not work.

five

It's All in Your Mind

M Y HIGH SCHOOL HAD SOME INTERESTING CHARACTERS on the coaching staff. One such character used statements that the team learned to both expect and ignore. Whenever a player was hurt he would say, "It's all in your mind, son." The alleged wisdom being, "It doesn't hurt that bad, so be tough and run it off."

When a player made a mistake, he would bellow, "Son, there you go thinking again!" The implication being, "You're dumb. Just do what I say." The coach was teaching young athletes that their minds were incapable of evaluating injury and remembering plays, that the use of their minds was an impediment to their success.

What he was right about in an indirect way was that in the majority of cases, the difference between success and failure is found between the ears, that life is "all in the mind."

Without question, the battlefield for anxiety is the mind. Anxiety is a strong inner pull in opposite directions. Expectations and reality are polarized; there is pain in the mind. Paul's prescription for peace is carried out in the inner sanctum of the mind.

According to Philippians 4:6, anxiety is the problem, and prayer is the alternative. Not just any old prayer will do. It is a prayer that is immediate and filled with thanksgiving and faith. The previously revealed prescription is as follows.

First, stop and pray. Second, give the anxiety object to God. Third, appropriate the peace of God and allow Christ to march guard duty around your life. But what if it doesn't work? This is the cry of many a well-intentioned believer who has struggled with the above process.

In the last chapter I gave five reasons why it doesn't work for many:

1. I did not think it would, which is a faith issue.

2. Fear that something more negative will happen, which is an emotional issue.

3. A physical reason, such as chemical imbalance, prescription drugs, fatigue, which is a medical issue.

4. Unresolved conflict with others, which is a relational issue.

5. Second-nature pathology, habitual negative thinking patterns, which is a thinking issue.

I will now add a sixth:

6. I did not want it to work.

This is a person afraid to change. Many are more afraid of change than of misery. Some self-destruct just before success comes because of their fear of change. The reasons for such an attitude vary—from poor self-esteem to "I don't deserve it; I should be punished," a feeling normally driven by guilt.

Without question, the most common and most difficult roadblock is number 5. The majority of failures in the battle against anxiety are because of deeply ingrained negative thinking patterns. Patterns are grooved into the mind and trigger conditioned responses. Often you react without thinking. This is because a particular event, smell, or sound triggers a programmed reaction.

When I was nine, I played in a piano recital. The piece was "Sleigh Bells" from *John Thompson, Book 1*. At age forty I still can play "Sleigh Bells." I no longer read music, I play no other songs, just this one. Why? I don't know for sure. But when I sit down at a piano and my fingers touch the keys, out comes "Sleigh Bells."

If one year's piano lessons could leave such an indelible mark, what about forty years of habits, attitudes, and practices? I drive in the right lane, I hold the phone in my left hand, I put my left shoe on first, shave the right side of my face before the left. These actions are taken without conscious effort. I get angry when I hear a certain voice and laugh at the sound of another. I get depressed, relieved, hurried, or joyful at various sights, sounds, and ideas.

You might fairly protest at this juncture, "If this is true, then what's the use? I'm helpless. I'm at the mercy of years of conditioning. I have no control over deep-seated habits." But there is good news: With God living in you, you can be more than an elite manifestation of Pavlov's dogs.

There is hope, but there is more to learn, so let's get started. Here is Paul's philosophy of learning:

> *Not that I speak from want; for I have learned to be content in whatever circumstances I am. I know how to get along with humble means, and I also know how to live in prosperity; in any and every circumstance I have learned the secret of being filled and going hungry, both of having abundance and suffering need. I can do all things through Him who strengthens me.*
>
> *Philippians 4:11–13*

"I have learned" in verse 11 is *mathetes*, in some places translated "disciple." Note the words and phrases: "I know how," "I have learned the secret," "I can do." What has Paul learned, what acquired skill does he claim that he "can do"?

Paul had learned contentment. By definition *contentment* is "a state of inner peace separate from circumstances." It would be synonymous with the peace of God mentioned earlier. This is clear in that both are internal in origin and separate from circumstance. This is the reason Paul can do anything; he has learned the secret. The word *secret* means something closed except for those privy to secret rites. The learned ability to make peace a part of daily life is secret except for those willing to follow Paul's prescription.

What is the secret to contentment? What we now know is that it was learned. It did not come overnight; he struggled to learn it. He tried and failed; he tried again and failed again, all the while making progress. God's peace didn't work for Paul for the same reasons it doesn't work for others. The seeker must first learn the secret.

Learning begins in the mind. Anxiety is an issue of the mind. The battleground for anxiety is the inner thought world, an arena filled with ideas. Therefore, the key to change is in the mind.

The mind has tremendous power; it is a marvel unequaled in manufacturing. It is the most complex mechanism in the world. Although it weighs a bit more than three pounds, it has 12 billion cells and 120 trillion connections. If the mind were a computer, it would be the size of the Empire State Building. It supervises everything from heartbeat to the most studied decision. While the heart, hands, feet, and legs wear out, 90 percent of the brain is unused.

Those who learn to tap the resource of the mind do remarkable things, both good and evil. How you use your mind determines not only attitude, but physical health as well. What the mind harbors, the body manifests. One medical doctor identified fifty-one diseases that come from anxiety. Eighty percent of illness is emotionally induced as it affects the lungs, the heart, liver, stomach, and colon. Everything from tooth decay to bad breath was mentioned.

The Bible supports the importance of the mind. "For as he thinks within himself, so he is" (Proverbs 23:7). Ideology dictates behavior. There should be no doubting that the mind is the key to change. Yet how to use it to effect the change remains a mystery to many.

Psychologists have studied it; pathologists have dissected it; people are baffled by it. Modern technology is trying to simulate it. But it can't be duplicated, simulated, or understood; only one person understands the mind of man, and that is the Maker of the mind.

"The heart is more deceitful than all else and is desperately sick; Who can understand it? I, the Lord, search the heart, I test the mind, even to give to each man according to his ways, according to the results of his deeds" (Jeremiah 17:9, 10).

If you desire to use your mind to its maximum, to utilize its power and creativity, then you had better listen to the mind's Creator. Understanding and managing the mind without God's help has led to the hodgepodge of differing theories called psychology.

While psychology has provided humankind with some helpful insights, on the whole, it has missed the mark.

The troubled mind needs change. The Bible refers to that change as a mind transplant. There are varieties of minds: creative, scientific, closed, inquiring, criminal, business, dirty, philosophical, strong, photographic, and encyclopedic. One fact often forgotten is that the human mind is limited, particularly with respect to spiritual life. The mind without the help of God is a terrific tool that draws the wrong conclusions.

The Bible teaches that the non-Christian mind is sick (Jeremiah 17:9), depraved (Romans 1:28), blinded (2 Corinthians 4:4), futile (Ephesians 4:17). It is unresponsive to spiritual truth and unable to understand it. The genesis of changing the mind is conversion. The person committing to Christ receives a new inner person that helps in renovating, rebuilding, and reprogramming the old mind.

We cannot possess a perfect mind in this life, but we can achieve what the Bible calls "the mind of Christ" (1 Corinthians 2:16).

The Mind of Christ: What Is It?

1. A Spiritual Mind (1 Corinthians 2:16)

The mind of Christ is a product of the Holy Spirit. Just as in the old axiom, "You can't get there from here," the road to a spiritual mind must pass through the Holy Spirit's terrain. The exhortation to possess a spiritual mind is found in Paul's Philippian letter.

"Have this attitude in yourselves which was also in Christ Jesus" (Philippians 2:5).

The Greek word translated "attitude" here is *phronema*. It can be translated "mind," but attitude is more accurate. An attitude is a mind-set, a way of thinking, a world view.

Phronema is again used in Romans. "For those who are according to the flesh set their minds on the things of the flesh, but those who are according to the Spirit, the things of the Spirit. For the mind set on the flesh is death, but the mind set on the Spirit is life and peace" (Romans 8:5, 6).

The objective of the mind transplant is to get into your mind what Christ had in His. This mind of Christ will make it possible for the Christian to live effectively and that includes anxiety management.

The mind transplant, being a spiritual surgery of sorts, begins with an incision. The incision is a decision, an act of the will. You see a need to change and, with determination, you say, "I want to learn contentment and I will take action." Once the incision is made, the reprogramming begins. And the reprogrammer is the Spirit of God.

The reprogrammer's process is described.

"For to us God revealed them through the Spirit; for the Spirit searches all things, even the depths of God" (1 Corinthians 2:10).

The antecedent *them* is the unknowable truth (v. 9) that cannot be discovered even by the most talented sleuth. It is a mystery that even Sherlock Holmes would not have the foggiest notion how to solve. A mystery that relinquishes not to investigation but to revelation alone.

This truth is not discovered, but revealed. "For who among men knows the thoughts of a man except the spirit of the man, which is in him? Even so the thoughts of God no one knows except the Spirit of God. Now we have received, not the spirit of the world, but the Spirit who is from God, that we might know the things freely given to us by God" (1 Corinthians 2:11, 12).

Only the Spirit of God knows the thoughts of God. Only the Christian has the Spirit of God. Therefore, only Christians can know the thoughts of God.

The purpose of the spiritual mind is that Christians might know the things God wants them to know. As a matter of fact, God desires that Christians understand Him so much, that He gives it away. *God is willing to give away His secrets.* Yes, even the secret to contentment, to the peace of God.

God is not playing "I've got a secret; bet you can't guess what it is." Instead, it's "I've got a secret, and I want you to know it." God desires that every believer can say with Paul, "I've learned the secret to contentment." Paul learned the secret and he tells us that the Spirit is the teacher. Not only is spiritual truth revealed by the Spirit, spiritual truth is taught by the Spirit.

"Which things we also speak, not in words taught by human wisdom, but in those taught by the Spirit, combining spiritual thoughts with spiritual words" (1 Corinthians 2:13).

The Spirit's task is to take the thoughts of God and get them into the minds of man. The means of communication the Spirit employs is the medium of language. The spiritual truths of God are communicated by spiritual words. The Holy Spirit utilizes the symbols of oral and written language to teach truth to His students. The truth of God in written form is the Bible. The first step, then, to acquiring the mind of Christ is to realize that the mind of Christ is a spiritual mind. Therefore, the transplant is a spiritual process.

The key to contentment is being Spirit-filled yourself. This is followed by the obedient step of seeking God's truth by regular exposure to the Bible. The right kind of information must be placed into the mind in order to learn contentment.

The right information is the first part of the process. The right content is a beginning, but it's not enough. In fact, the mere possession of truth alone can lead to disaster. Information without application leads to the common evangelical malady called *spiritual schizophrenia*, a spiritual split personality. The spiritual schizophrenic is an expert on what he is not experiencing. He is a hearer of the Word, but not a doer. His life is checkered with guilt and frustration. There is no sadder sight, and no more pathetic emotional state to be in, than that of a defeated, guilty Christian.

In fact, the greatest danger facing Christianity is not liberalism, communism, liberation theology, pornography, or other real and present evils in society. The more devastating danger is millions of professing Christians who are living testaments to the superficial and duplicitous nature of Christianity.

They possess all the trappings and can mouth the right words in the right order, but the reality is not there. There must be more; those dedicated to learning the secret and finding the peace of God must go a step further. The mind of Christ is not only a spiritual mind, it is a discerning mind as well. There are steps you can take to possess a discerning mind.

2. A Discerning Mind

The ability to think through the terrain of your life and apply spiritual truth is essential. Paul describes this ability vividly in the context of spiritual conflict.

"We are destroying speculations and every lofty thing raised up against the knowledge of God, and we are taking every thought captive to the obedience of Christ" (2 Corinthians 10:5).

How do you decide what is right about the shady stock deal, the kickback on a real estate project, the material used in construction, the claims on your tax form, what films you see, books you read, how you order your time, or where you live? On what basis can you take every thought captive to the obedience to Christ?

I liken it to a biblical defense system, or grid, where the unwanted ideology is strained out from the wanted. The Christian has a responsibility to build a defense system composed of God's thoughts about life. This is best done by systematic study of the Scriptures, which leads to thinking in categories concerning various subjects.

The result would be a defense posture on such subjects as abortion, infanticide, divorce, finance, physical exercise, politics, and so on. When an idea comes to mind, it is either accepted or rejected by our biblical straining system.

The reason so many are destroyed by anxiety is that they are defenseless in the war of ideas. Their minds are ideological war zones without defense. They are unwalled cities, open to any and all ideological assaults.

Television and other forms of media are the dominant teachers and mind shapers. Through drama, comedy, and music, they powerfully portray and preach an anti-Christian philosophy of life. They give the average person much to worry about.

If life's answers are not spiritual, then they must be political. Therefore, the government, politicians, and the happenings in Washington, D.C., are the most important workings of man. A nuclear arms agreement `is the hope of mankind. This is all presented with the underlying assumption that God is providing no meaningful answers and He is not in control.

On a more personal level, the media has taught `Americans, in particular, that we deserve only the best and has redefined *need* to be "greed." We need it because we want it. This breeds ingratitude, impatience, a desire for what we can't afford, and finally, a tendency to blame it all on someone else for not providing.

This kind of thinking is a hothouse for anxiety. When 95 percent of what people hear is this seductive anti-Christian philosophy, without a biblical defense system, they are in a helpless state. Anxiety will attack in great waves fueled by the ideology of the flesh.

There must, therefore, be a resolute effort on the part of Christians to learn the Bible and to make every effort to build a defense system that will protect them against the onslaught of wrong thinking.

But there is more to a discerning mind than content. The mind makes its discernments based upon experience as well as knowledge.

"But solid food is for the mature, who because of practice have their senses trained to discern good and evil' (Hebrews 5:14).

After a knowledgeable mind is seasoned in spiritual conflict, it will be trained to discern good and evil. This will not only be in the arena of ideas, but the motives and attitudes behind the ideas.

The mind of Christ, then, is both a spiritual mind and a discerning mind. The spiritual nature and the skill to discern make it possible for the third and vital characteristic to become a reality. This third dimension is the quality that conquers anxiety.

3. A Disciplined Mind

Christ demonstrated great mental discipline: The discipline to obey His Father's will regardless of internal and external militants. This is the reason Christians are exhorted to "have this attitude in yourselves that was also in Christ Jesus" (Philippians 2:5). Because it leads to obedience and the fulfillment of God's plan. The mind of Christ is a disciplined mind. It can see through the fog of relativism and the shaky moral atmosphere of modern life.

Since Paul is the author of Romans, Ephesians, Colossians, First and Second Corinthians, and Philippians, it is legitimate to combine some of his thoughts into a theology of thinking. He recommends a mind transplant in Philippians 2:5, explains the process for acquiring the mind of Christ in 1 Corinthians 2:9–16, and calls the Christian to have a focused mind in Colossians 3:2.

The main thrust, however, in rearranging thought patterns to overcome anxiety is our basic text in Philippians 4:8.

> *Finally, brethren, whatever is true, whatever is honorable, whatever is right, whatever is pure, whatever is lovely, whatever is of good repute, if there is any excellence and if anything worthy of praise, let your mind dwell on these things.*

The exhortation is a command, not a suggestion. The way to experience the peace of God is to train your mind to think a certain way. All minds are trained. Some are programmed for failure, some for success.

A businessman was driving between appointments late at night in an isolated area. To his dismay, he had a flat tire and no jack. His quick perusal of the landscape yielded no cars, no cities, only a single light in the distance. He began to walk toward that light. As he walked he began to think of all the reasons the owner of the house in the distance would not help him. He wouldn't open the door late at night, he would shoot him for trespassing, he wouldn't loan him a jack. His thinking continued to deteriorate. *People don't help like they use to; his jack won't fit my car; he won't even let me use his phone.* By the time he knocked on the door he was thoroughly convinced the farmer would turn him away. The farmer opened the door and the tired businessman yelled, "I didn't want your stupid jack anyway!" and stomped off into the darkness leaving a confused farmer wondering if he was dreaming.

Some people think the worst and expect the worst because they have been trained by others or by themselves to make anxiety a way of life. They quote axioms such as, "A pessimist is an optimist with thirty years' experience." They pride themselves on being realistic, pragmatic, and down-to-earth when what they really are is negative.

Compare this to one of President Reagan's favorite stories of two boys forced to shovel out a barn long overdue for a cleaning. One was frowning and grumbling as he halfheartedly dug at the manure and old straw, and the other was whistling a tune as he worked happily away. The first boy finally threw down his shovel and said, "I can't stand this! I quit! How can you work so hard at such a stupid job?" The other boy didn't stop digging as he answered, "There's got to be a pony down here somewhere!"

One was an optimist, the other a pessimist. Why? What is God's desire for the mind? Does He want Christians to be positive or negative? *God wants positive minds that are realistic without being pessimistic.*

A realistic, positive mind sees the good in life while not ignoring the bad. The positive mind sees the fingerprints of God all over life. In art, music, the purity of love and self-sacrifice, the honor of a soldier, the nobility of a nurse, the community worker. It takes note of the excellence in business, academic endeavor, good weather, the beauty of creation, and the benefits of liberty.

It is a mind that has been *trained* to see the good in life. The negative mind does not see or rarely sees the good in life. It has been trained to focus on what went wrong and what will go wrong.

Paul says the only way out of an anxiety-ridden life is to train your mind to focus on the positive and the good. When my wife and I attend a basketball game, we each see different things. Being a former cheerleader, she notices the kinds of cheers being done, the dress of the cheerleaders, and how these compare to an earlier time. The basketball game is superfluous. It's just ten men in their shorts trying to put a round ball in a basket.

But I, a former player, see the one-three-one-match-up zone, the screening and rebounding technique, and the coaching moves that determine the outcome. My mind is trained to see these finer points of basketball, hers is not.

The shoe is on the other foot when we stroll through an art gallery. While I can appreciate art, I know nothing of the details or finer points. I move quickly, finish the tour, and try to find the coffee shop. Jane stops and marvels at the abilities and techniques of the painters. Being an artist herself, she understands. Two different people, two different minds, trained to see life through different lenses.

Some people can filter the good from the bad in life, most cannot. A disciplined mind is trained to *focus on the positive aspects of life while not ignoring the bad.*

If you want to overcome anxiety, acquiring a disciplined mind that has the ability to filter and focus is not optional, it's a requirement. Most troubled people are anxiety plagued because their minds are undisciplined. Unable to focus, their minds run willy-nilly, like a mouse let out of a cage, speeding off without direction, out of control.

How then do I learn the secret to contentment? you ask. How do I get a mind transplant, take on the mind of Christ?

Before we answer this question fully, there is one important factor to consider. Don't make the mistake of believing that you have the power to transform your negative mind into a positive disciplined mind. It will require a Spirit-powered faith because a balance of positive thinking and reality is necessary.

You cannot ignore the facts of life. Former President Nixon ignored the facts of public opinion and the moral expectations that Americans have for their elected officials and left office in disgrace. Some faulty philosophies teach denial of the facts by simply pretending that you are somewhere else or that you really are not sick, bankrupt, fired, or in jail. This is foolishness, not faith.

The reason a Christian can filter the good from the bad, can focus on the positive amidst the negative, is faith. Faith in God and His goodness and power, not in ourselves and our ability.

Remember what faith is: "Now faith is the assurance [substance] of things hoped for, the conviction [evidence] of things not seen" (Hebrews 11:1).

The assurance or, literally, substance, is who God is, His character, goodness, the fact that He is in control. It's the confidence that "we know that in all things God works for the good of those who love him, who have been called according to his purpose" (Romans 8:28 NIV). The Christian's confidence is based on who God is, not on who we are or on our circumstances.

The conviction, or evidence, is the flawless track record that God has in the believer's life. It's the many times God has come through based on a promise in His Word. Therefore, Christians can be encouraged by the substance of God, the hope that He gives, and the evidence He gives through His faithfulness to His obedient children.

There does exist, though, something I call the "sabotage factor" in Christians who, because of their disobedience, have curtailed God's work in their lives. Their perception of God's track record is flawed because of a lifetime of short-circuiting God's entrance into their lives. They don't think God has come through, that He is good, that He cares, that He can or will do anything about their plight. They are rooted in doubt, not faith. That can be changed. How is discussed in the next chapter.

God gives Christians the power to be positive, to see life through the lens of Scripture, to see God's purpose and wisdom in what happens. God gives Christians the hope and power to build disciplined minds. A disciplined mind is trained by the Spirit. It is a spiritual mind and a discerning mind. It can filter the good from the bad and then focus on the positive aspects of life that free a person from the yoke of anxiety.

Now let us return to the question asked earlier: How can I get the mind of Christ?

The Mind of Christ: How Do I Get It?

How do I transform a fleshly, nondiscriminating, lazy mind into a spiritual, discerning, disciplined mind? What is the secret?

The first step is renewal of the mind.

"And do not be conformed to this world, but be transformed by the renewing of your mind, that you may prove what the will of God is, that which is good and acceptable and perfect" (Romans 12:2).

Transformation means change. The word is *metamorphoo*—"to be transfigured." The same root word is translated "metamorphosis" and used to describe the transformation of a caterpillar into a butterfly. All Christians are in a constant process of change. Hopefully, the change is from what a Christian is like to what Christ is like. The change is from a mind that is negative to one that is positive, from lazy to disciplined.

The syntactical relationships point out that the transformation is dependant on an outside force. That outside force is the *renewing of the mind*. To renew means to bring something into use that is dormant, to give new life to something that is tired.

Paul speaks of renewal in his second letter to the Corinthian church. At the end of the third chapter he is speaking of transformation. "But we all, with unveiled face beholding as in a mirror the glory of the Lord, are being transformed into the same image from glory to glory, just as from the Lord, the Spirit" (2 Corinthians 3:18).

"Therefore, since we have this ministry, as we received mercy, we do not lose heart" (2 Corinthians 4:1). He goes on to speak of the difficult obstacles he faced in spiritual leadership:

> *We are afflicted in every way, but not crushed; perplexed, but not despairing; persecuted, but not forsaken; struck down, but not destroyed; always carrying about in the body the dying of Jesus, that the life of Jesus also may be manifested in our body.*
>
> 2 *Corinthians 4:8–10*

God's people bounce. You can get up again and again from short-lived defeats. A great running back is not considered a failure because he gets tackled. Greatness results from how hard it is to bring you down and how fast you get back up again. A few defeats do not lose the war, the issue is whose team you are on and who wins in the end. Christians bounce back because they are being renewed by an unlimited resource that will win in the end.

Paul concludes his treatise on resiliancy with a great statement,

"Therefore we do not lose heart, but though our outer man is decaying, yet our inner man is being renewed day by day" (2 Corinthians 4:16).

Twice Paul ties the words *not losing heart* with *transformation* being accomplished by *renewal*. The Christian experience is the constant polarization of the body decaying, getting worse and worse, but the inner person being renewed and getting better and better. If the inner renewal is not taking place, the flesh wins and dominates the inner person. The cares and concerns of the flesh cause the Christian to accept anxiety as a way of life, and there is no defense.

Therefore, the mind must be renewed, making transformation possible. Thus far we know that a mind transplant is needed in order to win over anxiety. That transplant is called transformation—or change. The change takes place through a supernatural process called renewing of the mind. There are two steps to renewing the mind.

Step 1: Reprogram the Mind

The first action is to reprogram the mind with new information. That information is the Scripture. The reason the new information is needed returns us to the issue of many people being defenseless in the war of ideas. The call to Christians is to take ". . . every thought captive to the obedience of Christ" (2 Corinthians 10:5). And, of course, it returns us to the urgent need to learn the secret to the peace of God by acquiring the mind of Christ.

The Christian needs to understand the truth about history, its beginning, and its end; about God's world view concerning man, family, finances, government, war, poverty, hunger, and so forth. Therefore, you need to work at getting that correct information into place. That means Bible study.

Most Christians do not think christianly about life. They divide the secular from the sacred. They have yet to move their thinking out of neat little compartments and integrate it into all of life. Therefore, one ethic applies to "church life" and another to "business life";

one ethic to family, yet another to football. The result is an *informational ignorance.*

In July 1876 General George Armstrong Custer lay naked on the plain of the Little Big Horn with a single arrow through his heart. Why? Because of ignorance. History records that if a delivered bulletin had been heeded, Custer could have avoided the defeat. Many Christians have met defeat as a result of ignorance of the facts concerning their rights and privileges as Christians.

First, the right information must be placed into the human computer called the mind. Step 1 alone, however, would lead to the malady I call spiritual schizophrenia, which I described earlier. This unseemly condition makes exceedingly beautiful Christianity into something exceedingly ugly. It is Christians knowing what to do, but not doing it. It is what is commonly called hypocrisy.

Step 2: Apply the Information

Step 2 is the secret Paul wants all Christians to know, the secret that will unlock the door to the peace of God, contentment, and freedom from anxiety:

Renewing the mind begins with the right information, but its success depends on the practiced application of that information.

Biblical truth is more than theory. It is true even if it is not believed or practiced. However, for it to be experienced truth, to be meaningful to the Christian, it must be practiced. The cure for spiritual schizophrenia and the key to learning contentment is to translate theory into practice.

The renewing of the mind, then, is more than filling it with the right information—no one is tranformed by mere information. Let me explain the inner workings of the renewal process.

Once again Paul teaches us: "And for this reason we also constantly thank God that when you received from us the word of God's message, you accepted it not as the word of men, but for what it really is, the word of God which also performs its work in you who believe" (1 Thessalonians 2:13).

"Performs its work" is one Greek word—*energeo*—from which we derive our word, *energy*. It means to effectively act, work, operate, or produce an effect.

This verse has given rise to the animation doctrine. To *animate* means to give life or to fill with breath. Many relate it to animated cartoons in which objects not truly alive are made to appear to have life. What Paul is saying about the Word of God is this: The words written on a piece of paper are not alive, but the meaning behind these symbols, called words, are alive. The writer to Hebrews give credence to this fact:

"For the word of God is living and active and sharper than any two-edged sword, and piercing as far as the division of soul and spirit, of both joints and marrow, and able to judge the thoughts and intentions of the heart" (Hebrews 4:12).

The words come to life when, by faith, we read them and believe them. They are placed into our mind's computer. The renewing of the mind begins when, as stated in Step 1, you start reading, studying, memorizing, and meditating on God's Word. Your mind is exposed to a new set of ideas; you begin to take on a new world view.

Then comes Step 2, when you decide to take action. By faith and an act of your will, you put a new piece of information into practice. This is where the Word of God comes to life when energized by faith in action. Then the experiential ignorance is cured, as well as the informational ignorance.

For years you have believed that it was all right to lie. But new information has come into your mind concerning the importance of telling the truth. The conflict arises when it would be to your favor to lie. But the mind has been informationally renewed, therefore, you take action by faith and tell the truth. Now you have crossed the chasm that separates the immature Christian from the mature Christian. You have applied the Word of God, it has become animated, it is real to you now. It has become a conviction; your mind has truly been renewed with respect to the evils of lying and the advantages of truth telling.

That is true transformation, that is change, that is a mind transplant, that is learning the secret. For once you have learned the secret to transformation, you can change anything in your life through the power of Christ.

That is exactly what Paul meant when he said, "I can do all things through Him who strengthens me" (Philippians 4:13). I have learned contentment, I have learned the secret to the peace of God.

The renewal of the mind, then, is a two-step process

of, first, placing the right information in the mind and, second, applying that information by faith. The truth comes to life, or is animated and energized, by faith and the Spirit of God, then the transformation takes place in that particular area of my life.

There is another passage in Hebrews that puts this process together quite nicely.

> *For everyone who partakes only of milk is not accustomed to the word of righteousness, for he is a babe. But solid food is for the mature, who because of practice have their senses trained to discern good and evil.*
>
> *Hebrews 5:13, 14*

The reason for spiritual immaturity is one Greek word translated into two English ones: *not accustomed*. The literal reading is *without experience*. The cause of spiritual immaturity is a lack of practicing the principles found in the Word of God. Immature believers are not experienced with respect to the word of righteousness. This means they are not renewing the mind with the Scripture, neither are they applying it to their lives.

The cure for this pathological state is found in Hebrews 5:14: "But solid food is for the mature, who because of practice. . . ." The reason for spiritual immaturity is a lack of practice and the cure is a life of practice. Practice will bring about the desired result, which is a trained Christian. This text confirms what we have already seen is the secret to contentment: transformation by the renewing of the mind.

"I've learned the secret," claims Paul. The secret is that change is translating theory into action. If I transform my mind, I will transform my life.

Is that it? you ask. I just read the Bible, believe it, and then apply it, and I will have the peace of God? Well, yes and no. You can't go straight to application and have it last. Remember how Paul put it: I have *learned* contentment, I have *learned* peace, I have *learned* to overcome circumstances, I have *learned* to put off the old ways and put on the new ways.

Too many Christians fail because they expect the years of deeply ingrained negative thinking patterns to fly away as soon as they start renewing the mind. It will take time to make these new ideas a way of life. You can learn to manage anxiety by practicing the process of peace. Let's now review that process and add one more step.

1. Stop and Pray

The moment an anxiety object enters your mind, don't wait, stop and talk to God about it. Your eyes need not be closed, body posture is irrelevant—just do it. There is nothing so simple to understand, nothing more difficult to practice for the anxiety ridden.

2. Give It to God

Imagine in your mind's eye placing the anxiety object into the extended hands of God. Give it to Him for, after all, He asked for it. "Casting all your anxiety upon Him, because He cares for you" (1 Peter 5:7).

3. Allow God's Peace to Guard Your Mind

Thank God for giving you peace. Focus on the fact that Christ Himself is marching guard duty around your thoughts, your mind. Since the battle is one of the mind, Paul tells us that Christ guards both hearts (emotions) and minds (thoughts).

4. Read Your Blessing List

This is how to make Philippians 4:8 a reality: Whatever is true, . . . honorable, . . . right, . . . pure, . . . lovely, . . . of good repute, . . . excellence, . . . worthy of praise, let your mind dwell on these things.

The disciplined mind will be able to focus on the positive and the good. It will be able to filter out the good from the bad and then focus on the positive as described in verse 8. This does not come naturally, only supernaturally. Therefore, the blessing list is a tool to make this kind of thinking a reality.

The blessing list is a list of what is good about your life, those things for which you can be thankful. Your health, steady job, faithful spouse, loving church, and so on. Write them down on a three-by-five-inch card and slip it into your purse or shirt pocket. Put the card on the sun visor in the car, on the mirror in bedroom or bathroom. Then use it.

Whenever an anxiety object enters the mind, follow the first three steps, then pull out your blessing list and read it. Go over it two or three times. This will help you respond as you should, even though your thought process hasn't been changed yet.

Change the list twice a week to help you keep track of other positive things in your life. This may seem somewhat contrived, but it is a simple plan that has worked for hundreds of people. It is training you to follow a simple step-by-step plan to learn and make the process of peace a regular part of your life.

It will make practicing the process of peace as second nature as many other habits, good or bad, that are already established in your life.

5. Repeat the Process as Often as Necessary

Keep doing it, practice it for a period of six-to-eight weeks, and it will begin to be ingrained in your thinking.

Paul has told the reader to "think on these things," and there is one more crucial step to making the peace of God a lifelong possession. That step is practice. The nature and importance of creating lasting change is linked to practice. The next chapter considers the nature and importance of practice to the process of peace.

Study Questions

1. What are second-nature issues and why are they, by far, the greatest problems we face in dealing with anxiety?

2. To what does Paul refer when he says, "I have learned the secret"? What does learning have to do with the secret?

3. What is the battleground for anxiety? Where does learning begin?

4. Why does the unregenerate mind find dealing with anxiety a highly difficult task?

5. What is the mind of Christ?

6. What are the two steps to getting the mind of Christ?

7. Rehearse the five-step process of God's prescription for peace. Name each step and explain it.

six

Practice, Practice, Practice

W HAT COMES TO YOUR MIND WHEN YOU HEAR THE word *practice*? It depends, doesn't it? Your age, background, interests, all dictate what practice means to you. You may practice physical routines to stay young, to hold off the inevitable deterioration of your body. If you are a parent you might think of driving—to ball practice, trumpet lessons, dance.

Children practice eating, walking, talking, saying *mommy*. We practice spelling, basketball, singing, knitting, skateboarding, and medicine. When I launched my preaching ministry, I practiced with an ironing board as my pulpit. My wife would sit in front of me with a pad and pencil to critique me—with her back to me so she wouldn't laugh!

We are creatures of habit, and regardless of our like or dislike of practice, we do it all the time. We practice a certain style of thinking, speaking, walking, eating, and working. We get out of bed at a certain time, follow the same routine, same breakfast, same route to work, same greetings to the same people at the elevator, street corner, and lunch room. We come home and throw our stuff in the same place, eat at the same time with the same people, watch the same news show, and go to bed at the same time. Practice does not make perfect, but it does make a habit.

Habit is both positive and negative. Habits can lead to great success or drag one down to complete failure. For some, practice leading to a habit is their best friend, for others their arch enemy.

The Bible has a great deal to say about practice. Habit itself is amoral, it is simply a vehicle that is either a blessing or curse. Hebrews 10:25 teaches that it is a habit for some not to attend worship. It is something that is practiced over and over until it is woven into the life pattern. It is not surprising, then, to learn that the last and vital part to our prescription for peace is practice.

"The things you have learned and received and heard and seen in me, practice these things; and the God of peace shall be with you" (Philippians 4:9).

Like the imperative, ". . . let your mind dwell on these things" a verse earlier, "practice these things" is a command of equal stature. Learning the secret to contentment and the peace of God is a two-step process of, first, renewing the mind with information and, second, applying this knowledge. The mind is filled with new information through study, but the responses to life must be reshaped by practice.

An interesting twist to the text is that peace is promised when you stop and pray and, in thanksgiving, give your anxiety object to God. This is clear from 4:6, 7. This is the supernatural, nonsensical, incomprehensible peace of God in that moment. It is the peace of God for that moment, but not on an ongoing basis.

It is a new experience, not a habit, not a regular part of your daily life, but it is promised through practice. ". . . the God of peace shall be with you" (v. 9). The peace of God will be part of your everyday life if it is practiced into your way of life. Paul has commanded Christians to practice "these things." These things refer to the prescription for peace found in 4:6–8. Make them part of your life, do them over and over again until they are second nature. In this case, practice makes permanent.

Let's explore the nature of practice, *why* it should be done, and then *what* should be practiced.

Why Practice?

Why should a football team practice? Because practice leads to learning and improving skills. Because practice leads to change, to a trained team. A well-trained team will play well and get the maximum from their ability.

Another way of saying the same thing is that the team changes from the time it starts training camp till the first game. That change is improvement in conditioning, skill, and teamwork.

The goal of a Christian practicing certain things is to change for the better. The goal is change, arriving at what the Bible calls a trained Christian.

Let's take a closer look at the reasons for practice.

1. Practice Is the Heart of the Training Process

This is clearly taught by the writer to the Hebrews. "For everyone who partakes only of milk is not accustomed to the word of righteousness, for he is a babe. But solid food is for the mature, who because of practice have their senses trained to discern good and evil" (Hebrews 5:13, 14).

The metaphor of *milk* is employed to teach that immature Christians are not ready for and cannot handle the responsibilities of spiritual adulthood. More important than the description of spiritual immaturity is the reason for it. The reason some Christians are not mature is that they are untrained.

The root cause of their immaturity was that they were "not accustomed," from the Greek word *apeiros* meaning "to be without experience." They were without experience with respect to the "word of righteousness," that is, scriptural truth. They had not practiced the principles in the Word of God.

They were not involved in the two-step process of the

secret, namely, renewing the mind with information first and application second. In fact, the author implies they were stagnant, unproductive, and apathetic. They were not practicing the process.

The mature, on the other hand, can handle solid food. They are growing, maturing, and are ready for the responsibilities of spiritual adulthood; they are trained. Our word *trained* in Greek is *gumnazo*, from which we derive our words *gymnastics* and *gymnasium*.

The mature are in this good condition "because of practice." The reason for spiritual immaturity is a lack of practice, and the cure is a great deal of practice. Practice is essential to good training. A gymnast may practice six hours a day, six days a week to be trained. A typist may practice twenty minutes a day and be considered trained. Regardless of the acquired skill, *the principle of practice leading to training is absolute.*

The secret Paul speaks about is to take theory and translate it into action. There must be practice in thinking and doing in order to bring about lasting change. This is the reason for his command in Philippians 4:9 to "practice these things."

Another reason for practice is results.

2. Practice Yields Good Results

For the Christian to manage anxiety or anything else, for that matter, he must be trained. The virtue of practice is that it yields the desirable fruit of being trained. There are three aspects that are important to our discussion of the trained condition.

First, as it relates to the Word of God.

"All Scripture is inspired by God and profitable for teaching, for reproof, for correction, and training in righteousness; that the man of God may be adequate, equipped for every good work" (2 Timothy 3:16, 17).

While the word *training* appears in this text, it is the word *equipped* that demands attention. *Equipped* is from the Greek word *katartizo* and it has several possible meanings: to set a broken bone, mend a net, furnish a house, restore deteriorated material to original condition, or condition an athlete. Clearly it means a work of restoration, building, and conditioning.

The Scriptures provide the basis for a four-phased process of restoration or building: teaching, reproof, correction, and training. *Teaching* explains what is true and right, it charts the course. For example, "be a truth teller" (Ephesians 4:25). *Reproof* is the rebuke of God's Word when one lies, ". . . he who tells lies will perish" (Proverbs 19:9). *Correction* teaches how to get back on the right track—repent, confess, accept forgiveness (1 John 1:9). *Training* implies the steady practice of being a truth teller when it costs one to tell the truth. Teaching, reproof, correction, and training are parts of a process charted by the Word of God. This process is necessary for learning and for Christian growth.

Expect this process to be alive and kicking in your battle with anxiety. You have your prescription, the course is charted for you. But then you fail, and the Word reproves you, tells you how to get back on course, and exhorts you to practice, practice, practice, and then practice some more. Like slowly restoring a dilapidated car to mint condition or setting a broken bone, the process takes time. This practice must continually take place via the Word of God, for the Bible provides a standard, a measuring stick, and a means for the equipping process.

The only way for a Christian to be equipped or trained is to begin with the Bible. This supports our earlier thesis: Change begins in the renewing of the mind with information first (Romans 12:2). That information is found in Scripture. Any meaningful training that leads to the management of anxiety will require a concerted effort to learn and apply Scripture to life. So, why practice? Because practice will lead to being trained or equipped. And equipping begins with the Word of God.

Another aspect to practicing and training is the influence of others. ". . . but everyone, after he has been fully trained, will be like his teacher" (Luke 6:40).

Fully trained is from the same word which was translated "equipped" in 2 Timothy 3:17—*katartizo*. The trained disciple will be like his teacher. This is both frightening and hopeful. This in part explains why Paul invited the Corinthians to, "Follow my example as I follow Christ's" (1 Corinthians 11:1 NEB). The "as I follow Christ's" served as a disclaimer. The duplication of undesirable parts of our nature is the frightening part. The reproduction of Godly traits is the hopeful part.

For practice to be really effective it must not only

possess the standard of the Word of God, but have models as well. The Word of God takes a person through the continuing four-part process, and it helps greatly to have a teacher. "The things you have learned and received and heard and seen in me, practice these things; and the God of peace shall be with you" (Philippians 4:9). If you want to learn golf, reading the rule book alone is not enough. Studying a book with diagrams would help, but without a teacher, chances of success are slim. We have, therefore, a need for the teaching golf pro. He not only reminds you of the rules of the game but also playing technique. He teaches, reproves, corrects, and trains you on the golf course itself. He does one other crucial thing: He can take a club in hand and demonstrate *how* it is done.

Your swing becomes much like your teacher's. You approach the game with the same philosophy, same temperament; you are like your teacher in many ways. There are many differences as well, but your teacher has had a great influence in your life. Practicing the prescription for peace is a teaching that will be much easier to follow with a fellow traveler, teacher, or both.

Personality is a product of relationship. This axiom is more important when speaking of anxiety. The teacher not only can remind the learner of the prescription for peace, he can also teach the struggler how to get back on course. The teacher will have struggles of his own that will serve as a helpful model.

A point of clarification: When I say prescription for

peace, I am referring to the five-step plan outlined by Paul in Philippians 4:6–9:

1. Stop and pray

2. Give it to God

3. Appropriate the peace of God

4. Read your blessing list

5. Practice, practice, practice

When I refer to the four-step process of training, I am speaking about the teaching, reproof, correction, and training process in 2 Timothy 3:16, 17. If you were to mix the five-step prescription for peace with the four-part process for training, all five steps of Paul's prescription would fall under the one category of *teaching* in 2 Timothy 3:16, 17.

There is one more element vital to the equipping process. The essential players thus far have been identified as the Word of God and a mentor/teacher. The third is found by continuing our trace of the word *katartizo*.

"And He gave some as apostles, and some as prophets, and some as evangelists, and some as pastors and teachers, for the equipping of the saints for the work of service . . ." (Ephesians 4:11, 12).

Again the word *equipping* is from *katartizo*. The third

major player in the equipping process is the corporate body of Christ. It includes the variety of gifts, exeriences, and challenges found in a commitment to a group of believers.

The above text is the only guarantee for corporate maturity found in the New Testament. Gifted leaders in the Body of Christ are to coach (train) the saints (average believers) to do the work of ministry. This text assumes the priesthood of all believers and that everyone who knows Christ is a called and set apart minister of Christ with a role to play and a gift to exercise.

Equipping is best done when all three major players are working in concert. The Word of God, the mentor/teacher relationship, and the resources and dynamic of the corporate body of Christ. These three players represent the necessary ingredients to equipping. Practicing requires a plan, that is the Word of God. It requires accountability and modeling, therefore, the teacher/mentor. It requires variety of experiences and challenges: enter the corporate body of believers.

Practice is the key to being trained. That is why Paul exhorts the Christian to "practice these things" (Philippians 4:9) with respect to anxiety management.

Practice is vital because being trained is a basis for Christian maturity and Godliness. ". . . discipline yourself for the purpose of godliness" (1 Timothy 4:7).

Perhaps you have attempted to practice new habits, to change undesirable traits. Like a locomotive stoked and ready to move, you were filled with eagerness. But just as a locomotive without rails churns into the ground, you found yourself deeper in the mire of unwanted habits. What rails are to a train, discipline is to practice. When you practice with eagerness, discipline provides the means of moving toward the goal of being equipped. Being equipped makes it possible to manage anxiety and practice the peace of God.

Godliness, maturity, being equipped or trained, experiencing transformation, having learned the secret to contentment—these are the direct results of practice. The equipped Christian will find applying scriptural truth natural because he has become adept through practice.

A person who reads music and plays the piano has mastered the basics of musical skill. The learning of additional instruments becomes easier because the basic skill and knowledge has been learned. Likewise, if you have overcome anxiety by learning the basic skill of putting off old habits and replacing them with new habits, you can change your habits in other areas such as eating, anger, and bodily disciplines. There are few limits to your ability to change.

Let's review the thesis for change. The vehicle for transformation or change is the renewing of the mind (Romans 12:2). Renewing the mind begins with information first and then application follows. Renewing the mind starts with the right information, but its success depends on the application of that information. The application comes from the practice of the principles learned. That continued practice leads to an equipped or trained Christian who is mature.

Your motive for reading this book is probably a desire to change, or to help another change, or to learn more about the nature of change.

The Nature of Change

Many people think that if they stop doing something they have changed. Although ceasing certain activities is helpful, this is a half-truth. The Bible describes change as not only stopping one behavior, but replacing it with another behavior.

> *That, in reference to your former manner of life, you lay aside the old self, which is being corrupted in accordance with the lusts of deceit, and that you be renewed in the spirit of your mind, and put on the new self, which in the likeness of God has been created in righteousness and holiness of the truth.*
>
> Ephesians 4:22–24

You will note the familiar exhortation to "be renewed in the spirit of your mind." The means for renewing the mind, which is the key to transformation or change, has been firmly established in earlier chapters. The nature of change which calls for clarification now is putting off and putting on aspects. More will be said later, but the nexus for now is that change has not occurred until a new mind-set and behavior has replaced the old.

Let's say I want to lose weight. There are various diets available. There are many plans that will lead to weight loss, but most, however, do not lead to change. The vast majority of dieters lose weight on a special plan, only to regain the weight after the diet goal is met. The reason is simple: If old eating patterns are not permanently replaced by new patterns, you will revert to the old.

The new habit pattern must be practiced in order to replace the old. *Real transformation and change are the products of disciplined practice over a period of time long enough to form new habits.* This is the case not only with eating, but with anxiety, as well.

The answer to the question, "Why practice?" should be obvious by now. Simply put, practice is the key to lasting change. Disciplined practice will put off old patterns and replace them with new patterns. The old pattern is negative thinking that leads to anxiety; the new pattern is the prescription for peace revealed in Philippians 4:4–13.

The exhortation of Paul was *"practice these things."* The answer has been provided to the question, "Why practice?" Now the issue is *what* to practice. How am I going to put feet on these principles? How can I make anxiety management work?

What to Practice

Paul commands Christians to "practice these things." Paul's prescription for peace must be practiced to be

175

firmly entrenched in daily life. The five-step prescription for peace, if practiced properly, will make victory
over anxiety possible. There are six principles to follow
in your practicing, and they apply to winning over
anxiety or any other change that you desire. These
principles will make it possible for you to practice the
prescription for peace long enough to make it work.

1. Get Insight Into What Must Be Changed

Insight is the capacity to discern the true nature of a
situation. In the spiritual realm, it is to see the world
and ourselves as God sees—to look at life through His
eyes, or the lens of Scripture. Again Paul instructs us,

> *I now rejoice, not that you were made sorrowful, but
> that you were made sorrowful to the point of repentance;
> for you were made sorrowful according to the will of God,
> in order that you might not suffer loss in anything
> through us. For the sorrow that is according to the will
> of God produces a repentance without regret, leading to
> salvation; but the sorrow of the world produces death.*
> 2 Corinthians 7:9, 10

To see our sin as God sees it will bring deep sorrow.
That sorrow will lead to repentance, and repentance
means change. Our word *repent* is derived from the
Greek word *metanoeo* meaning to "turn about, or change
your mind."

It is not uncommon for a person to practice something

176

for many years and not realize its destructive nature. You get up in the morning and, for the first time in years, take a good look at your body in a full-length mirror. In that moment, the mirror reflects back to you the evidence concerning years of self-abuse. The reality hits you in a way that is new and different, and you experience remorse, shame, regret, anger. This is insight. You have seen your condition for what it is, deplorable. Then repentance comes, you change your mind and determine to change your life-style. This is the genesis of change, this is where victory begins. Repentance is the starting line for change.

Insight, then, is to see our sin as God sees it and to repent, turn around and desire a different attitude or behavior. In this case, insight means to see the destructive nature of anxiety as described in chapter 1. After insight, I am moved to change, which is repentance. I am ready to put off the old and replace it with the new.

What is it that must be changed? Often the problem seems too powerful and big. Like trying to tackle an elephant, you grab on only to be run over. Therefore, the problem that is to be solved must be cut down to size. So the approach is to dissect what is happening. What is the nature, frequency, and occasion of my problem?

What is the nature of it?

What am I doing? What am I feeling? Let's say I am depressed. I feel blue; I don't want to work or be with people. Sometimes I don't care to get dressed or take care of basic grooming needs.

What is the frequency?

How often is it taking place? Daily, hourly, constantly, mornings, afternoons, evenings? My answer is, every evening when I am preparing dinner for the family. The problem is not cooking—I love to cook. It is not the children—I don't have any. It's not the aroma or the work in the kitchen. But the frequency is daily around 6:00 P.M.

What is the occasion?

What triggers it? If I keep a daily log for one week, the cause of my depression becomes quite clear. Every evening during this time my mother calls and grills me concerning the events of the day. The tone of her voice and the guilt-producing questions take me back to childhood and remind me of my inability to please and perform up to her standards. This sends me into a downward spiral and only a good night's sleep can pull me out.

I get depressed daily at 6:00 P.M. when my mother calls. There is a problem cut down to size. Once we find a pattern there are a number of actions we can take to break it.

Insight into what must be changed is the key to solving any problem and will cut it down to size. It may be arguments that lead to depression, phone calls that incite outbursts of anger, or seeing someone who brings back a painful memory. Even eating certain foods or experiencing particular smells can throw a life into imbalance. Try to identify the source.

2. Find an Alternative

After you discover what needs to be *put off*, the next step in making a change is to find what needs to be *put on*. When is a liar no longer a liar? If you answer, "When he stops lying," you are half right. The better answer is, "When he becomes a truth teller," when he has *put off* lying and *put on* truth telling.

Examples of alternatives abound in Scripture; here are a few.

"Now flee from youthful lusts. . . ." This is the practice to be put off. ". . . pursue righteousness, faith, love and peace, with those who call on the Lord from a pure heart" (2 Timothy 2:22). This is the behavior to be put on.

"Let all bitterness and wrath and anger and clamor and slander be put away from you, along with all malice." This is to be *put off*. "And be kind to one another, tender-hearted, forgiving each other, just as God in Christ also has forgiven you" (Ephesians 4:31, 32). This is to be *put on*.

Whatever the problem, you will want to find the biblical alternative to the negative attitude or behavior. With respect to anxiety, you want to *put off* worry and *put on* prayer. *Put off* negative thinking and *put on* positive thinking. *Put off* passivity and *put on* practice.

Put off the years of negative thinking and practice that have damaged you and start to rebuild by putting on the peace of God. You put on the peace of God by consistent practice of the five-step prescription for peace.

If you cannot seem to find the biblical alternative, get some help. There are people who can find it for you. Don't give up simply because of a lack of information. You can get that by asking people who know the Bible.

3. Prepare Yourself for Change

Let's say you have experienced insight concerning a negative attitude or behavior. You have repented and determined to change. You have found the biblical alternative. You are ready to put off the old and put on the new. You attempt to put off and put on, but you fail. The reason? You did not restructure your life for change.

You wanted to stop smoking, but you kept the cigarettes in your coat. You wanted to lose weight, but the candy and ice cream are still in the refrigerator. You are fighting depression, but you stayed in bed and did not follow the new schedule. You wanted to stop doing drugs, but you still go to the same places with the same people and willpower is not enough.

Many changes must be made in order for the practicing of new patterns to benefit you. This is the reason for the halfway house for released prisoners, drug addicts, alcoholics, and other addicted persons. The halfway house provides structure and encouragement to facilitate the change.

If you are trying to manage anger, you had better structure your success by concrete actions such as writing yourself notes to remind you what you are to do. Have your plan for counteracting the anger ready to go, whether it be push-ups, running, hitting a mattress, or woodworking. Just have it ready to go so you can put off the old and replace it with the new.

In the same way, anxiety management means to structure your life for success. Have the process written down. Have your blessing list with you and updated. Make sure that your activities, surroundings, and associations are consistent with your desire to change.

People, places, and situations that are anxiety builders should be avoided. It should be admitted that the majority of anxiety builders cannot be avoided, but you would be surprised how many can be. Even if 25 percent of anxiety builders could be avoided or eliminated, it would assist your healing.

4. Learn How to Break a Habit

Even after insight, repentance, the discovery of the biblical alternative, and the major restructuring of your life, success is reduced to breaking habit patterns. This will not happen in a day, a week, or even a month. It will take consistent practice over a period of months to put off the old and replace it with the new.

The first order of business is to understand the nature of breaking patterns. There are two levels at which the battle is waged: resistance and restraint.

Resistance: This is always the preferred method of winning, the easiest as well. James advocates it: ". . . resist the devil and he will flee from you" (James 4:7). Two immediate benefits are derived. First, you don't engage in sin; second, the devil temporarily leaves you alone.

The best method of fighting sin is to resist it at the temptation level. Instead of anxiety, stop and pray, give it to God, appropriate His peace, and walk in the power of the Spirit. That is effective resistance.

While *resistance* is the preferred method, it is rarely practiced. It is with *restraint* that the majority of people are waging war.

Restraint: Most people start with *restraint* in overcoming anxiety because the propensity to worry is so deeply ingrained. Before you know it, you are engrossed in worry. It came so quickly. Without warning it flooded your mind. Therefore, learning to chip away at its power is the work of restraint.

We must develop the right attitude about restraint. Some of us find it hard to even admit that the battle is at restraint more than at resistance because the very idea that anxiety or other problems have that strong a hold on us makes us feel like failures. My studied opinion is—*Hogwash!* We must accept the reality of life. We must struggle. We must fight and establish a beachhead from where we are, not from where we wish, hope, dream, or think we ought to be. To be enmeshed in the battle is not failure, it is the bumpy road to success.

The fatal flaw is to think, *Oh, dear, I broke my diet and ate a piece of pie. Oh, well, I might as well make a night of it and have it á la mode.* Is it more of a sin to eat the pie á la mode than the plain pie? Yes, yes, yes. Three or more times, *yes*. If you can't resist, *restrain*. Restraint is simply to retreat and hold your ground. Don't desert—no pun intended.

There are several biblical injunctions that teach restraint.

"The beginning of strife is like letting out water, so abandon the quarrel before it breaks out" (Proverbs 17:14).

Just because *some* water has escaped the spigot, don't turn it on full-blast, turn it off. It's rarely too late for holding back, stopping, or restraining yourself from further action.

"A fool always loses his temper, but a wise man holds it back" (Proverbs 29:11). Years of bad habits are difficult to break. Habits with regard to restraint of negative emotion can determine the label given you, wise man or fool. The wise man has learned to restrain himself, the fool has not.

When there are many words, transgression is unavoidable, but he who restrains his lips is wise.

Proverbs 10:19

He who restrains his words has knowledge, and he who has a cool spirit is a man of understanding.

Proverbs 17:27

> *The heart of the righteous ponders how to answer, but the mouth of the wicked pours out evil things.*
>
> Proverbs 15:28

The goal is resistance, but if we lose there, we must immediately retreat and retrench at restraint. The core issue is to make progress. Paul told Timothy to let his progress be known by all men. The anxiety battle is one of learning the prescription for peace by practicing it into your life—by putting off the old and putting on the new. This is all God asks and all you can expect from yourself.

Change is a journey and some parts will be rough, testing all your resolve. Other days will be easy, providing the progress and encouragement so important to continuation. This is why Paul wrote in Philippians 4:12 that he had *learned* to be content. He had learned peace, the secret, because he had practiced for years.

Strive to stop and pray immediately upon the appearance of anxiety. This will give you some victories at the point of resistance. When you fail at resistance, which will be common early in the game, retreat and retrench at restraint. Work your way, then, backward from restraint to resistance. Reverse the flow. Your diligent practice will take you back to the front of the class which is resistance. Break the pattern of sin at resistance first, restraint second, then gradually reverse the trend. You can do it.

5. Accept Encouragement and Accountability

All progressing Christians need help. If you think breaking the anxiety pattern is a project for a loner, you are mistaken. You will need every bit of help possible to put off the old and put on the new. You will fall and stumble, you will need someone to pick you up.

"Brethren, even if a man is caught in any trespass, you who are spiritual, restore such a one in a spirit of gentleness; each one looking to yourself, lest you too be tempted" (Galatians 6:1).

People who care are vital to the success of other struggling believers. A loving Christian friend to restore your hope and your resolve to go on is basic to making change. Don't resist help, look for it, learn to appreciate it.

At other times, you will need ideas, someone to cheer you on, possibly to exhort you to go on.

". . . and let us consider how to stimulate one another to love and good deeds, not forsaking our own assembling together, as is the habit of some, but encouraging one another; and all the more, as you see the day drawing near" (Hebrews 10:24, 25).

This is the accountability aspect. Often the person trying to overcome a counterproductive habit pattern will start out with great vigor and determination. But the rigors of the warfare, the disappointments of losing at resistance and spending most of the time in the trenches of restraint, sap the vigor and erode the determination. It is exactly at that crucial moment, that the strong encouragement of a friend will hold us accountable to keep trying, to not give up.

Make a pact with a person you respect and trust. Tell him what you are doing, create a checkup system, and make him promise to hold you accountable regardless of your avoidance or resistance to this accountability. This will facilitate your progress greatly. It is an often-overlooked step in making important life changes.

6.   Don't Forget God

The captain of a great ocean liner had begun as a cabin boy years earlier and gradually worked up to his high position. He had become one of the most respected men on the high seas. His assistant, who had served with him for years, observed and emulated his every move. But one thing about the captain puzzled him: Every morning the skipper went to his cabin, opened the top drawer of his desk, took out a small slip of paper, read it with intense concentration, returned the paper to his desk, and locked the drawer.

After many years, the captain retired and his assistant took command. The first thing he did was open that drawer to discover what was on that slip of paper. The paper had but one sentence on it: "*Port* is left; *starboard* is right."

Don't forget the basics, the obvious reasons for success. Don't forget prayer, Bible reading, spending meaningful time with other Christians, and sharing your faith. These will keep your spiritual life alive and provide the most important means to success: the ministry of God's Holy Spirit. Remember, no spiritual process, including the prescription for peace, will work without spiritual resource. You can't wire around the Spirit of God.

7. Practice, Practice, Then Practice Some More

The number one reason for failure is that people give up too soon. Whether it be a diet, an exercise program, learning speed reading or golf, most people simply don't stay at it long enough to acquire the needed skill. This is certainly true of the battle to beat anxiety.

It will take nine to twelve weeks to put off the old habits and put on the new. The five-step prescription for peace must be diligently practiced for three months. Faithfully practiced for three months, this prescription will have worked into your life, it will be a new habit replacing the old.

Vince Lombardi, the great coach of the legendary Green Bay Packers, was reported to have said, "The will to win is everything." While I agree that the will to win is important, another great coach said it better. Bobby Knight, the controversial and temperamental coach of Indiana University basketball, said, "The will to win is not as important as the will to prepare to win." The will to practice is essential to winning over anxiety. The seven last words of the defeated Christian were, "I tried it, and it didn't work." Don't give up too soon. Practice the process. Let's review the process one more time.

1. Stop and pray (Philippians 4:6)
Instead of worrying, immediately stop and pray regardless of where you are or your circumstances.

2. Give the anxiety object to God (4:7)
Regardless of techniques used, give the object to God in prayer.

3. Appropriate the peace of God (4:7)
Appropriation of the peace of God means to believe by faith that God has taken the anxiety object. He has taken it, He can take care of it, and He is in control and has your best interests in mind. Even visualize Christ marching guard duty around your life.

4. Read your blessing list (4:8)
Read it; memorize it; have it near at all times. This will begin to rebuild the thought process; this is putting feet on the transformation. This is the development of the mind of Christ. This is putting on a new way of thinking.

5. Practice the process (4:9)
Practice, practice, practice, and then practice

some more. Don't give up; be determined. This will become part of your life in a period of nine to twelve weeks if practiced properly and consistently.

Don't give up too soon. You can't climb Mount Everest in a day. It will take some time, but it will be worth it. Remember the words of Paul as your goal:

I know how to get along with humble means, and I also know how to live in prosperity; in any and every circumstance I have learned the secret of being filled and going hungry, both of having abundance and suffering need. I can do all things through Him who strengthens me.

Philippians 4:12, 13

"I can do all things through Him who strengthens me."

And so can you.

Study Questions

1. What role does practice play in the training process?

2. What results does practice yield?

3. Name the three main players or elements in practicing.

4. Name the seven principles for change and then take each one and plan how you will deal with your own anxiety issues.

5. Develop a strategy for applying and using these principles.